Pepper
PEOPLE

Pepper PEOPLE

By Charles P. McCormick, Jr.

A **BENJAMIN** Book

Library of Congress
Catalog Card Number: 92-75558

Produced and published by
The Benjamin Company, Inc.
21 Dupont Avenue
White Plains, NY 10605

ISBN 0-87502-246-4

CONTENTS

Dedication

Charles Perry McCormick
1896-1970

With fond memories, this book is dedicated to Charles P. McCormick, former leader of McCormick & Company, Inc., my Dad.

Realizing that employees spend most of their waking hours at the work place, he dedicated himself to making those hours as productive and pleasant as possible and practical.

My father was known to his employees and friends as "C.P." or "Charlie" or "Mr. C.P." His vision created the Multiple Management philosophy that guides our Company today.

The inspiration for creating this book is derived from his everlasting humor through good times and bad.

When I was a kid, he told me, "Son, we don't make much money in this business, but we sure have fun."

Foreword

McCormick & Company has prospered for over 100 years as an independent food company. There aren't many independent billion-dollar food companies in the United States.

There has been one common thread that has been most important to our Company since the introduction of our Multiple Management philosophy in 1932. It is management's belief in the importance of the individual employee. One result of practicing this belief is the good humor that follows – as night follows day.

There has been such an abundance of kidding, needling, laughing, and just good camaraderie at McCormick that many former employees have suggested recording some of the humorous stories of our past. On the following pages, we have endeavored to do just that amid highlights of our Company history. Many of the most humorous stories are unprintable. What we hope to have recorded here are memories in some good taste. Some of the others would certainly not be well received by some of our very conservative Baptist forebears. We hope that we have achieved a happy compromise in our selection of anecdotes. We wish to offend no one. On the other hand, to those of you who occasionally have a sly smile on your face, enjoy.

To those present or past McCormick employees who are not mentioned in this book, I apologize. To those of you who *are* mentioned, I apologize even more! Without you, however, and without those of you who contributed those stories, there would be no book.

PEPPER PEOPLE

Special thanks go to Jack Felton and Jim Lynn for editing, and to Theresa Capel, whose organization of these many stories made *Pepper People* a joy to write.

Pepper
PEOPLE

Chapter One

Detroit 1950

"Get it off me! Get it off me," the man screamed from the next bed.

It was 4:00 A.M. in a hotel room in Detroit, Michigan. It was Thursday night, the last night of a long week for the sales crew from Baltimore and other parts of the country. For the first time in the history of the Company, we had descended on the Motor City to launch McCormick spices.

Four years earlier, we had launched our attack on Chicago, and in just one year, we had become number one in the Windy City. Chicago later became our first million dollar sales market. In Chicago, when we had said we represented McCormick and Company, the reaction was generally, "Are you selling newspapers or tractors?" The *Chicago Tribune* McCormicks and the McCormick Harvester McCormicks were famous there, but nobody had heard of McCormick spices. In Detroit it was the same. Nobody had ever heard of us.

So it was an assortment of sales executives, old-time peddlers, and eager, young World War II veterans who had returned to start their careers. I was the youngest in the crew at age 22. Three years earlier, I had been a member of the Chicago team – *after* we became number one. Let me assure you that I wasn't ready for the hard sell that was necessary in downtown Detroit.

The "Get it off me" call came from my roommate.

Unlike me, he was a dynamite sales executive from our Washington, D.C. district. He had had the best record all week in selling new accounts and was thoroughly enjoying the experience – day and night!

PEPPER PEOPLE

While I needed eight hours' sleep and probably more because of my lack of sales success, Jim Philbin was on a sales high that warranted only a few hours of sleep each night.

Struggling to respond to his call for help at the ungodly hour of four in the morning, I couldn't find a bed lamp. Finally I hit the light switch which engulfed the room with brightness. I *couldn't believe* what I saw.

There was a hat on the floor, but no other clothing. All the rest was in the bed – suit, shoes and overcoat. Jim was dressed just as he had been when he left the last watering hole.

What was even more bizarre, Jim was wedged between the mattress and the box spring! It must have taken an immense burst of "alcoholic" energy and power for Jim to get into bed by lifting up the mattress and neatly and quietly sliding himself between it and the box springs.

But at six-thirty that morning, Jim jumped up all bright-eyed and was off again. He sold three more new accounts before the weekend came!

McCormick wins again!

Chapter Two

Willoughby

It was the month of September 1889 when Willoughby M. McCormick began manufacturing operations in Baltimore in one small room and a cellar, plus a backyard used for storage. He employed two women. Almost every morning after he had arranged the production schedule, he would call on the trade with his samples and gather in more orders. Sixty years later, sales executive Ole Olson would proclaim, "Nothing happens until you get an order." Willoughby McCormick must have known this inherently.

Willoughby was so successful that the business moved to larger headquarters seven times in four years. From humble beginnings, in just two decades the Company became important in its industry. Back then, practically all of the country's food supply was controlled by wholesale grocery houses, which distributed packaged goods under their own private brands. As always, the blight of the price cutter was a burden to honest merchandising. But in those days, price was more important than quality. Willoughby, being of Scottish descent, knew how to pinch a penny and did.

His big rolltop desk was stuffed with used paper that still had enough room for a new message to be written on the back or in a corner. Used and bent paper clips filled several nooks. Nothing was thrown away.

In 1904, the great Baltimore fire consumed the major part of downtown Baltimore, and with it the McCormick building. The fire changed the course of McCormick's history and taught us a

Company founder, Willoughby M. McCormick, resurrected his young Company from the ashes of the Great Baltimore Fire of 1904.

major lesson. Although W. M. McCormick had earlier adopted the Bee Brand label as his own trademark, he had sold little merchandise with that identification. Ninety-eight percent of the firm's business was private label. After the fire, Willoughby realized that very little goodwill had been built with the consumer, and that many of his customers would not hesitate to switch suppliers while he was attempting to rebuild his plant.

With the advent of another new plant, Willoughby selected Bee Brand as his consumer label. Willoughby stated, "One of the cleanest and most valuable of insects, the bee is discriminating; it selects the best for its production. A bee is courageous and remarkably industrious. Our Company entertains visions of developing a vast industry where the wheels would hum as do the bees in a hive."

I am constantly asked by new acquaintances where I got the nickname "Buzz." It happened in the hospital shortly after my birth when a nurse, aware of the McCormick connection with Bee Brand, called me Buzz. Because I was a junior, the nickname stuck.

Willoughby developed other brand names too, such as: Uncle Sam's Liniment –"fit for man or beast," Reliable Brand drugs; Iron glue –"sticks everything but the buyer," Queen Bee tonic and King Bee tonic; and Bee Brand shampoo –"good for dogs and humans."

The best-known slogan, still revered and carved into a beam above the Tea House fireplace at corporate headquarters, is, of course, "Make the best – someone will buy it." This slogan was developed late in Willoughby's years, certainly not in the early cost-cutting, price-focused days. (The truth of the matter is that C. P. McCormick developed the slogan and attributed it to his uncle.)

Willoughby built his factories and moved seven times before finally building, in 1922, the largest reinforced concrete building south of New York City, at 414 Light Street in Baltimore. Meanwhile, his sales force was also aggressively building new distribution.

Some of the sales tactics of the day were ingenious. Salesman Arthur Doherty was particularly successful in his Florida territory.

PEPPER PEOPLE

Doherty was a natty dresser. Along with his Panama hat and cane, he had a jacket full of appealing pitches for customers, but his ultimate tactic was reserved for the rare case of a total turndown. It was this: Doherty would stiffen up with a glazed look in his eyes, clutch his chest, do a neatly executed pirouette, and

Balto., Md., Feb. 8, 1904.

Mrs. R. B. McCormick,
    Middleburg, Va-
My dear Ma,-
         Enclosed please find check, but will ask you to hold this up for a few days until we find out whether or not it will be any good. We do not know how our money is, as it is tied up in the Banks which have been burnt.
        I am sorry to tell you that we lost everything, except our books, which we got out about 3 o'clock this morning. There was not a drop of water put on our building, the fire simply traveled so fast that we had to run for our lives. You cannot conceive of the awful calamity that we all have met with. From Howard Street to our old place is one great big sea of debris, some places on Balto.. street being two stories high with brick caused by the walls falling in. It will be years before we can recover our loss.
        We have opened up temporary quarters at Gay & Front Sts. and will start up in a humble way there again.
        I will try to keep things moving at home.
        Corrie will no doubt go home in the next few days, and Katherine will no doubt do likewise, and possibly it will be well for you to go back to Dover and keep your expenses down as well as possible until I can see where I stand.
        I will have what money we have on our books to start up again with, as for our insurance, we never expect to get much of it. Most of the Companies will fail. The losses are three or four hundred millons, and evn this will not cover all.
        I have met with a little misfortune in having my hand badly bruised, and cannot use it and of course it makes me quite nervous, as it is very painful, but I hope it will be all right in a short while.
        Give my love to Miss. Ida and keep up I am going to start again and will try to do my best.
        I do hope that Harvey is better, but by all means do not let this worry you. We have but one good Mother and we must keep her.

18

fall to the floor in a beautifully feigned heart attack. During the frantic minutes of getting water for the fallen Doherty and helping him to his feet, the grocer was greatly motivated to get Doherty out of his store without further exciting him. And thus, the sale was closed. It worked time after time.

This letter from Willoughby to his mother shows his concern for the welfare of his employees after the fire that destroyed most of downtown Baltimore.

One of the Company's earliest brands was Bee Brand. The bee was chosen as a symbol of purity, industry and cooperation.

McCormick's landmark Light Street building looked out over the Baltimore Harbor for nearly seven decades.

Uncle Willoughby passed away in 1932, when I was four years old. I remember him as a rather short man, impeccable in very formal business dress complete with vest, high collar, and stick pin. He lived in the stylish Warrington Apartments on North Charles Street. With his chauffeur, Charles Manokey, he rode to work for a number of years in his electric car (yes, they had them back then.)

Driver Charles Manokey, a highly educated and well-spoken black man, held a number of positions in the Company. After his formal retirement, Manokey managed the Company's main parking lot until age 98. Willoughby had promised him a job as long as he would come to work. Manokey came to work every day for seventy years and outlived three wives.

Willoughby hired young men to train for executive jobs. What this really meant was that they were paid a "trainee's wage." He also hired seven of his nephews, feeling he could pay them less by holding out the carrot of future responsibilities.

Only two of these nephews remained with the business, Charles P. and Hugh P. McCormick, Jr. These two were made to know that they were in training and that they were not to expect any special privileges because of their kinship.

Hugh, the elder of the two brothers, became deeply interested in the study of spices. Although his health failed in 1926, he went on to become Vice President, and was largely responsible for

Charles Manokey, Willoughby's chauffeur and the Company's oldest employee, retired in 1986 at 97 years of age.

building the Company's huge spice business. At the time of his death in 1936, he was considered the leading spice authority in the United States.

His son, also named Hugh, spent a successful career with the Company and eventually became the top executive in charge of all of our important government commissary business around the world.

The other nephew, C. P. McCormick, was fired at least seven times because of his frequent disagreements with the way his uncle handled people. In those days, one would certainly describe Willoughby as a highly successful entrepreneur. Like most entrepreneurs, as the business grew, Willoughby needed to temper his early displays of genius with new business methods suitable for a larger organization.

Willoughby's autocratic methods of operation were typical of businessmen of the times. He was authoritative – actually, a one-man show. Nobody made major decisions but he. The Board was passive and relied upon his judgment. He was a pillar of his church, helped found the Baptist retirement home, and gave generously to the University Baptist Church on Charles Street. After all, his brother, the Reverend Hugh P. McCormick (my grandfather) was a Baptist missionary. Willoughby was also one of the four Baltimore business leaders who founded the Community Chest, later called the United Way.

On the other hand, employees resented the fact that Willoughby did not pay a decent wage. After Willoughby's death, when C. P. McCormick became President, one of his small, but nice, innovations was to present a fresh turkey to each employee at Thanksgiving. This was prompted by C.P.'s knowledge that most of our employees could not afford a family turkey at Thanksgiving. Most had to cook a much less expensive and less meaty goose. The tradition of the gift of a Thanksgiving turkey to each employee continues today.

In the Willoughby days, new employees moving to Baltimore from out of town were sent to the YMCA to find temporary living quarters. Bill Karl, the personnel manager, sent newly hired Ted Rodgers uptown for this purpose. By mistake, Ted entered the

McCORMICK BLOCK.
(OFFICE, PRATT AND CONCORD STS.)

GOLD MEDAL GIVEN "BEE" AND "BANQUET" BRANDS EXTRACTS, SPICES AND TEAS AT JAMESTOWN 1907.
CABLE ADDRESS - "McCORMICK"
A.B.C.CODE, 4TH AND 5TH EDITIONS AND PRIVATE CODES

McCORMICK & CO.
INCORPORATED
IMPORTERS, EXPORTERS & GRINDERS
DRUGS, TEAS, SPICES, &c.
MANUFACTURING CHEMISTS

EXPORT OFFICE:- 116 BROAD ST., NEW YORK
PHILADELPHIA OFFICE:-7 S. FRONT ST.
NEW YORK OFFICE:-100 HUDSON ST.

MEMBERS
NATIONAL ASSOCIATION OF CREDIT MEN.
CHAMBER OF COMMERCE OF THE U.S.
FLAVORING EXTRACT MANUFACTURERS ASSN. OF U.S.
AMERICAN SPECIALTY MANUFACTURERS ASSN.
NATIONAL WHOLESALE DRUGGISTS ASSN.
AMERICAN SPICE TRADE ASSN.

BALTIMORE, MD. 1/9/15

Mr. D. S. Green,
100 Hudson St., New York City.

My dear Mr. Green,

I note your letter to Mr. Bond this morning, in which you state that you are somewhat disappointed in the matter of your salary.

For three months hand running we have been sinking money pretty heavily. The war has cost your firm many thousands of dollars and we have had on our staff several men who have been losing money for us for months and we cannot help ourselves, as it has not been their fault, but the conditions have been against them.

Now this is a give and take institution and always must be. We have not seen daylight yet in New York, but I am not at all discouraged. We want to pay our men every cent that is coming to them, but even so, our men sometimes will have to sacrifice some profit in order to tide over those who are causing us loss. This is always the way - sometimes you must push up and sometimes pull up. It is a struggle all the time and we are doing our very best for our employees.

I am perfectly satisfied to eat humble pie this year, because I know that most manufacturers have lost very heavily. No doubt you have noticed that a good many of them have already closed their shops and retired from the field, but we don't want to do that.

I simply write you this letter to encourage you. I think you have done exceedingly well considering the times and conditions in your city. Keep a stiff upper lip and I am sure you will come along all right. It may take another six months or a year before things come your way, but we believe they have just got to come that way before long. People are getting low in stocks and I am glad to say orders are coming in very well indeed. with kindest regards and best wishes, Sincerely yours

CORRESPONDENCIA EN ESPAÑOL
CORRESPONDANCE EN FRANÇAIS
CORRESPONDENZ IN DEUTSCH

WMM/W

This letter from Willoughby attempts to motivate a disheartened salesman during tough times.

YWCA. When he asked for a room, the lady at the desk smiled and surprised him by asking if he wanted one or two ladies as roommates?! That might be possible today, but not in the 1930s!

Despite a certain pompousness, and his high profile as a leading churchman, Willoughby was observed on occasion strutting

*Willoughby's brother, Roberdeau McCormick,
the Company's vice-president.*

uptown himself to take in the afternoon show at the famous Gayety Burlesque Theatre, part of Baltimore's notorious "Block."

In those days, the phrase "alone at the top" was a remarkably apt description for a business owner.

One of McCormick's early consumer product successes was mayonnaise.

If salesmen today did what was prevalent competitive practice in the 1930s, they would undoubtedly, if caught, end up in jail. In the fight for shelf space, it was a common trade practice to remove the lid of a competitor's mayonnaise jar and insert a little piece of dirt in the product before rescrewing the cap. The result in a few days was a badly discolored product which, of course, didn't move off the shelf. Neither did all the good packages sitting behind it. For the faint-hearted salesman, merely unscrewing the competitor's closure just enough to admit air into the package also created a slow death for the competitive products.

In his later years, Willoughby, of course, did not call on the trade as much, but there's a great story handed down from a salesman who took Willoughby on a sales call. Willoughby talked to the customer about everything but business, which was never mentioned . . . not even once. After the call, Willoughby said to the McCormick salesman, "If you ever have any other tough nuts to crack, let me know!"

As the stock market crash of 1929 and the Depression that followed took its toll, Willoughby's management methods became even more tight-fisted. Several times each day, he would tour the facility to make sure everyone was working. Knowing this, the employees set up a communication system. From the moment Willoughby walked out of his glass-walled office, signals were sent throughout the building using every form of plant communication known, from vocal – "The old man's coming" – to fast beats on production pipes with a hammer. Twice a day, every day, every employee in every department worked like hell.

Willoughby was also innovative. One Thanksgiving and Christmas season the plant was not very busy. Willoughby decided that he would give a number of the younger fellows a chance to continue earning their salaries through an unusual method.

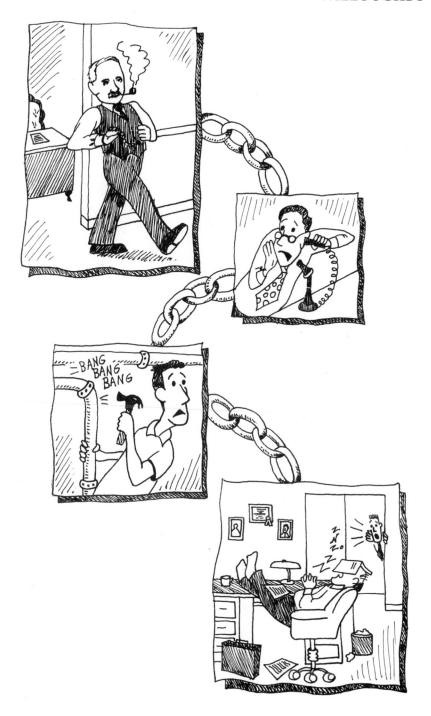

"C. P." succeeded his uncle Willoughby McCormick. It was C. P.'s philosophy that created Multiple Management.

He made arrangements with a number of grocery stores in the suburban areas of Baltimore who were good McCormick customers to give our men market baskets filled with McCormick spices and extracts. The young men were told to go to houses near the store and knock on doors and offer the spices and extracts at special prices to the people who lived there. It was a success, and created a new sales technique known as "market basket salesmen." (Now there's a new idea for our McCormick/Schilling Division if things really get tough.)

Insecticides were an important line of products during the early years. Later, during World War II, McCormick supplied most of the lice powder that was a necessity for our troops living in fox holes. The early Bee Brand line of dry powders and liquid fly sprays was especially popular in the South. Much of the product was sold out of small drugstores. Here again, each salesman had his own marketing technique.

Sales crews would invade the South early every spring and load up accounts with a year's supply of ant powder, roach killer, fly spray, and pump guns for the spray. C. P. McCormick had a sales technique that worked well. As he approached the store to be called on, he would find a little kid on the corner. C.P. would give the youngster a nickel and instruct him to earn it by going into the store and asking for Bee Brand ant powder. A few minutes after the kid came back out, C.P. would enter the store, introduce, himself and proclaim, "I'm sure you are getting many requests for my products."

I guess a nickel meant a lot to a kid in those days, particularly when you consider that Willoughby's normal tip for an overnight pullman porter consisted of pressing a tea bag into the porter's outstretched hand and then thanking him profusely for the courteous service.

In 1932, while on a trip to New York City, Willoughby McCormick died. The business had been losing money because of low sales during the Depression. Employee wages had been cut twice; on his deathbed, Willoughby ordered a third cut. The purpose of his trip was to raise money for the floundering business. With its founder and president gone, morale was lower than most bank accounts. McCormick & Company was in trouble.

C.P., age 36, was asked to take over the troubled Company.

Chapter Three

Charlie McCormick (C.P.) and His New Business Philosophy

One of the great McCormick peddlers still recalls the first time he met C.P. McCormick, then President of the Company. During a sales meeting dinner in Dallas, Texas, one "Red" Elliott stepped up to Charlie and introduced himself. Red said, "I'm glad to meet you, Mr. McCormick," and drew the reply, "My father was Mr. McCormick. Just call me Charlie."

This illustrates the personality of the person whom the Board of Directors elected in 1932 to replace Willoughby McCormick as President.

As his oldest son, I remember one thing above all about him: his kindness. Now mind you, he could get quite excited and angry once in a while. But deep down was a basic love for his fellow workers, which exhibited itself in myriad ways. He was creative (he could have made a living as an artist), spontaneous, innovative, definitely a maverick, unselfish – and he had a flair for doing the unexpected.

I was reminded recently by a longtime employee that "C.P." often carried hard candy in his pockets, which he liked to give to little kids. Serving as a member of the regional Federal Reserve Board gave him the idea of giving all McCormick employees' children silver dollars at Christmastime, and no one enjoyed it more than C.P. This also became a Company tradition.

C.P. faced seemingly insurmountable odds at age 36. As the newly elected president of a troubled company, he bravely introduced a brand-new philosophy for doing business, and with it, a new management system. He reversed his Uncle Willoughby's decree for a third wage cut. Instead, he raised wages by 10 percent! He cut the workweek hours, threw out all time clocks, and proclaimed that from that day on, "We will replace fear with faith." He also initiated profit sharing. Employees were encouraged to purchase Company stock, and plans were set up to help them do so. This would no longer be Willoughby's business; it would be an employee business. People were indeed more important than machines.

His new business philosophy was called Multiple Management (management by many). Its birth was derived from Charlie's deep appreciation of team sports and his belief that good teamwork was stronger than an assemblage of superstars.

Although not a religious man to the same degree as his Baptist minister father, he had learned some basic lessons well. His business philosophy was built on these beliefs:

First was the Golden Rule: "Treat others as you would like to be treated." Charlie carried this further with his proclamation to employees that "the Company will think twice for you and once for itself. In return we expect you to think twice for the Company and once for yourself." This became known as the "2 for 1" spirit.

Employees were told that in order to turn the Company around, nine needed to do the work of ten, but that all would share in the rewards of success – much like the New England whaling crews who shared in the catch. One should not forget that these fresh ideas were advanced shortly after C.P.'s election, and just as all banks were closed by executive order.

Within a year, the Company was in the black again, and it has been every year since. The new participatory philosophy has grown into a strong culture. The Multiple Management Boards created from it are still the backbone that makes this culture unique and so successful.

C.P. loved to work hard and play hard. His type of leadership had an immediate impact on morale, motivation, and alertness. His mind was quick and unexpected, so you could never make book on what his reactions might be.

The same Red Elliott who learned quickly to address him as

Charlie had an even more important meeting with him later. You see, Red's boss decided to fire him, and he sent Red to see C.P. in Baltimore in order to make the action final. After hearing both sides of the controversy, C.P. instructed Red's boss not to *fire* him, but to *train* him. Red is still an important sales executive.

C.P. also liked practical jokes. One was to carry a pair of scissors and cut off an unsuspecting executive's tie. Normally this happened just when the executive was feeling important over some success. Tie-cutting had great shock value the first time, and certainly stimulated some mixed reactions. However, without fail, a brand-new, expensive tie was always presented as a replacement the next day.

C.P. also discovered that by grabbing a collar tab on a formal shirt, one could actually tear the collar right off. At one of his annual New Year's Eve parties, he greeted each male guest by tearing his collar off. You can imagine the ridiculous look of forty men dressed to the hilt in formal attire, all with their collars missing. This was during World War II, when white shirts were hard to come by. But miraculously, the destroyed shirts were also replaced by C.P.

During the 1940s, we were one of the first manufacturing companies to make use of a professional psychological consulting firm: Rohrer, Hibler and Replogle (RH&R) of Philadelphia. Dr. Charles Flory, our original counselor, remembers his first trip to McCormick headquarters, then located in downtown Baltimore.

He entered the lobby and was greeted by C.P. They both got on the elevator to go to the seventh-floor offices and were joined in the elevator by one of the great old characters of the Company, Buck Burton. Buck, who headed up the shop, was a jolly guy and a favorite of C.P.'s. He always called C.P. "Mista Challey." He was a large, robust, pear-shaped man with a bald head. Buck always wore blue overalls with suspenders. The elevator girl (as we called them in those days) closed the door, and C.P. intrigued our new psychologist by pulling a large pair of scissors out of his coat pocket. While introducing the good doctor to Buck Burton, C.P. cut off Buck's suspenders. Buck's overalls fell immediately to the floor, to surprised looks from all on the elevator.

The only time I have seen this act eclipsed was when another Rohrer, Hibler and Replogle consultant was introduced for the first time to another all-time McCormick character, Bob Sharman, at a Regional Sales Managers' meeting at the Company's island retreat on the Chesapeake Bay. It was evening, and all of the regional managers were going to go through "shrink" sessions the next day with Dr. Flory's replacement, Dr. Jack Gillespie. Jack was taken around the room and introduced to the sales managers, many of them playing gin rummy. When they got to Sharman for his introduction, without looking up he said, "Can't you see I'm busy? I'll see you tomorrow."

Buck Burton

Bob Sharman and wife Gina.

Sharman tried to call me one night at 3:00 A.M. from a bar-room in Miami, and mistakenly got C.P.'s number. When C.P. tried to tell him whom he was talking to, he wouldn't believe it, and he gave the President a load of garbage for about five min-utes before realizing his mistake. He made no more early calls.

C.P. loved all of these characters. On another occasion, Buck Burton, dressed in his usual overalls, got off the seventh-floor elevator to find two visitors at the reception desk, but no receptionist. Buck asked the couple if he could help them. The man introduced himself with a formal British accent: "I am Lord Leverhume, the Chairman of Lever Brothers, and this is Lady Leverhume. We are here to visit Mr. McCormick." With that, Buck grabbed the shocked couple, one on each side of him, and down past the Friendship Court offices they went, arm in arm. As he wheeled them into the front office, he said, "Mista Challey, this here is Lord and Lady Leave-her-home." The Lord and Lady were both amused and impressed by this introduction, as well as by the room into which they had been brought (C.P.'s office was actually the Board of Directors' room).

Due to his participatory management style, C.P. usually had people in his office. He also liked to use the wall space to hang pictures of all of the Multiple Management Board executives as well as outside business acquaintances and celebrity friends such as President Eisenhower. C.P. vowed to make three new good friends a year from outside the business and professional worlds. Soon many faces were gleaming from the wall.

However, the focal point of the office/boardroom was a most unusual circular desk that was made to fit in one corner. Aside from providing a large flat surface where C.P. enjoyed doodling while talking or listening, it represented somewhat of a rebellion from the styles of his stern father and uncle. It looked more like a bar than a desk. When we opened our new corporate headquarters in Sparks, Maryland in 1991, the old desk was refurbished to take its place in the Chairman's office.

In 1934, a Tea House was constructed at the Light Street building. In his early sales days, C.P. had spent much time waiting in customers' offices or vestibules, many of them unpleasantly crowded, too hot, or too cold. During some of these waiting periods, he vowed that if ever given the chance, he would treat visitors and salesmen in a more gracious manner.

With this in mind, a replica of an "old English Tea House" was created in the seventh floor lobby. Visitors were served tea by young ladies dressed in long Elizabethan-period gowns, and business was often conducted in the Tea House rather than in the Company offices.

It became so popular that shortly after the Tea House was constructed, it was enlarged and became the center for an entire Shakespearean Street known as Friendship Court. This hallway separated various offices that had facades made to resemble old English houses, complete with thatched roofs. Decorating the stairs to the eighth floor, where the general office was situated, around the hall and up each wall of the McCormick Little Theater (seating 107) were murals done by local artist Edwin Tunis, who had designed the Tea House and Friendship Court. These murals depicted the history of spices and were preserved when the Light Street building was sold in 1989. Restored, they provide decor for the new corporate office building in Sparks, Maryland, which opened in 1991.

Later, the first-floor reception area at Light Street was decorated to look like an early pioneer cabin in Virginia, and additional murals were painted by Tunis for the Human Relations area. In keeping with C.P.'s proclamation, a large inscription over the Human Relations doorway stated, "To all who enter here, we pledge faith not fear."

Also at Light Street, a variation of the quote was painted on one of the boardroom doors: "Fear knocked at the door. Faith answered. No one was there." In Friendship Court, a "2 for 1" keystone was inscribed. This stone symbol of C.P.'s "2 for 1" people philosophy was eventually placed over the front entrance of the new corporate headquarters at Sparks.

McCormick was, and possibly still is, the only company to put Human Relations on its balance sheet – symbolically valued at one dollar, just like goodwill.

During the 1930s and 1940s, McCormick's chief chemist was a little bald-headed man with thick glasses by the name of Dr. John Glassford. He was a stereotypical absent-minded professor: brilliant, but often oblivious to what went on around him. He became the butt of every practical joker in the Company. Many used to delight at breaking an egg on Doc's head. Every time it

happened, Doc didn't seem to realize it until the egg started dripping down on his face. He would feel his head and exclaim, "Is that another egg?!"

When Doc was on C.P.'s boat one day, someone tied his suitcase to a rope, towed it behind the boat, and then told Doc to look at what had been done. Seeing the suitcase riding on the boat's wake, Doc thought this was hilarious, until he followed the instructions to pull it in and discovered it was his own suitcase.

C.P.'S NEW BUSINESS PHILOSOPHY

On another boat trip, Doc caught several fish. He proudly called his wife after the boat was docked to tell her to hold dinner, as he had fresh fish to fry. He had carefully wrapped them and put them in the top of his valise, which he left on board the boat. When he arrived home to present his fish, he unwrapped the package to discover not two fish, but two empty beer bottles. His wife accused him of being drunk.

For many years, an executive dining room was adjacent to the cafeteria. Many lunches used to end in a "war of rolls" being tossed around the room. Here again, Doc Glassford was the recipient of many jokes. He thrived on it; in fact, he felt hurt if ignored. At meals, he couldn't turn his head without garlic salt being put in his tea or his food being covered with ketchup.

At one Christmas party, held the morning of Christmas Eve for employees and their kids, Doc memorized a thirty-two-verse poem. He didn't get through the first verse before they started cutting off the microphone and turning it on and off at different levels. Everyone in the place was laughing hilariously, but Doc went through the entire thirty-two verses unfazed and unaware of the prank being played on him. On another occasion, Doc made a speech while firecrackers exploded beneath the podium, and the audience left one by one until only C.P. remained, with Doc rambling on as though nothing were happening.

One of C.P.'s talents was his ability to respond to new situations and turn a potential problem into a plus. One such occasion happened when two union representatives called on him and announced that they were going to unionize the employees. He greeted them with a smile and passed them his cigar box. He said, "I'll smoke my cigar while you tell me your story, and then you light up and I'll tell you mine."

When C.P. finished telling the union agents about his own people philosophy and the many benefits employees had, the agents stood up and one of them said, "Mr. McCormick, if all businessmen were like you, we would be out of a job. Obviously, there is nothing that we can accomplish here. God bless you."

Over the years, McCormick has acquired a number of companies that had union representation. In nearly all cases, plant

39

employees eventually chose to be independent of union representation. We're not anti-union; we just believe that we have always
had a higher interest in our employees' welfare than any outside
group possibly could.

C.P. felt that there were five important needs for an employee:
1) fair pay; 2) security; 3) opportunity; 4) participation; and 5)
recognition. Today, our human relations program still addresses
each of these needs.

With C.P.'s informal management style, there were few
departmental walls as far as he was concerned. If he thought of
an idea for sales, for instance, he might give it to the production
manager if he happened to see him first.

Employees quickly learned that C.P. was allergic to both garlic
and onion, two of our fastest-growing products. One morning, I
was sitting in the office of the Purchasing Director, Howard Wolf.
This was the first office off the elevator. The plant was filling garlic that day, and the smell permeated the elevators. C.P. departed
the elevator and wheeled into Howard's office on the way to his
own. He said, "Howard, did you smell that garlic on the elevator?" Howard said, "Yes, sir." C.P., in all seriousness said, "Then
why in hell don't you do something about it?" Howard looked
rather amazed and uttered another muffled, "Yes, sir."

One day, C.P. wrote to the President of Campbell Soup, suggesting that the onion be taken out of one of the soups: "Some
people don't like onion, and it can always be added but not taken
out." As he proudly reported this to some of his associates the
next day, he was told that we were the company providing the
onion for the soup.

C.P. felt that executives serving on Multiple Management
Boards spent many extra hours on business opportunities. He felt
strongly that not only did they deserve some rest and relaxation
time with their families, but it was necessary in order to keep
their thinking fresh. This was the reason an additional benefit to
serving on one of the Boards became the awarding of additional
vacation time, usually taken during the winter/spring months.
On top of this, a special bonus was provided to pay for the vacation. If no vacation was taken, no bonus was given.

For a number of years, most executives went to Daytona Beach, Florida during March or April. One evening about sixteen of us were there, including C.P., and he decided to treat all of us to steak dinners. He was so allergic to garlic that if a steak were even cooked on a surface that had been previously exposed to garlic, C.P. could tell.

Harry Wells, who later became Chairman of the Board, was sitting next to me. As my steak was put in front of me, I could smell some garlic. I said to Harry, "Watch C.P." When the waiter attempted to place C.P.'s plate in front of him, it reminded me of a pilot practicing takeoffs and landings. That plate barely hit the table before it was whisked off. Not only that, C.P. sent *all* the steaks back for garlic-free ones.

As the Company grew, C.P. became an important local business leader. Recently, former Judge Dulaney Foster told me of the time many years ago when he was talked into running for Mayor of Baltimore against the incumbent, Tommy D'Alesandro, Jr. Someone suggested that Mr. Foster visit C.P. to discuss his campaign.

C.P. had regularly paid Tommy D'Alesandro's filing fee, and also knew there was no way the astute D'Alesandro could be defeated. But C.P. welcomed Dulaney Foster and listened to his ideas. Finally, C.P. said, "Yes, I think you could have a chance to defeat Tommy. Let's go uptown to lunch and talk about it."

As they left the front door of 414 Light Street for the six-block hike through the produce section and business sections of downtown, C.P. said, "Dulaney, you know a lot of people. As we walk uptown and talk, do me a favor and give a little wave to everyone you see that you know." When they arrived at the hotel restaurant, C.P. turned and said, "Dulaney, you only waved at four people. You don't know enough people to get elected, and I suggest you drop out of the campaign." He did, and became instead a successful Circuit Court judge for Baltimore County, a position he held for thirty-five years.

C.P.'s belief in sports, teamwork, and unselfishness led him to initiate the McCormick "Unsung Hero" award for Baltimore high school students. An unsung hero from each high school football team was selected and recognized at a banquet totally sponsored by McCormick & Company. The concept was to recognize unselfish team play by saluting those who make the difference but normally lack recognition for their low-profile roles. For years, the banquet was televised, and originally it was held in the Light Street cafeteria. Top national sports celebrities have always been featured speakers.

One evening, as the crowd assembled in Friendship Court, a large fire broke out in the old piers on the other side of cobblestoned Light Street. The television crews assembled on the seventh floor to cover the banquet quickly turned their cameras to the fire and had instant live coverage of the disaster. The Fire Department, however, arrived quickly and put the fire out. Mayor Tommy D'Alesandro, always a supporter of the Unsung Hero Banquet, arrived in a fury and screamed, "We'll have to pay to tear all those old piers down and when we're lucky enough to receive the gift of a fire to do it for us, my idiot Fire Department puts the fire out!"

Another year when the mayor arrived, he was equally exasperated. There was a big controversy over some nude art in the city's art gallery. The mayor said, "If some poor little kid down on Albemarle Street has nowhere to take a leak and he goes on the curb, he's arrested and sent to jail. If such an act is painted in the art gallery, it's okay, because then it's art!"

Weeb Ewbank, Don Shula, John Unitas, Brooks Robinson, and many other sports greats have been entertained in the Crow's Nest after Unsung Hero Banquets.

One memorable Unsung Hero Banquet ended up with our speaker, Bill Veeck of baseball fame, entertaining until the wee hours of the morning. His stories were great, but it was disconcerting when he rolled up his pants leg and used his artificial leg as an ashtray. He had many operations which amputated a little more leg each time, and he made the best of it by having a custom ashtray built in, so that when he crossed his artificial leg, there it was.

The Unsung Hero Banquet has grown since 1940. In 1987, women's basketball was added to the football program. The

Banquet is now held in May instead of December. A college scholarship is awarded to each of the outstanding male and female "unsung heroes" in addition to the individual trophies presented to each school's award winner. Each scholarship is presented by the Board of Directors in honor of C.P. McCormick.

C.P had a special way of teaching things. I smoked one entire cigarette in my life. I was fifteen years old and sitting on the fender of a car on Charles Street. When I arrived home that night, my father met me at the door with a smile on his face. He said, "Son, I understand you are smoking. That's fine, but let me give you some advice. If you smoke, please do it at home; and always smoke cigars, because you don't inhale them and therefore, they're not as bad for you." With that, he shoved a cigar in my mouth and lit it. I smoked, choked, and turned green, and barely

The Unsung Hero Banquet has always been supported
by prominent civic and sport leaders. Baltimore Colt coach,
Don Shula, addressed the audience in 1965.

got past the first few puffs. He said, "That's all right, I'll teach you how." The next two nights, he also met me at the door, and we went through the same drill. The choking, sick feeling didn't improve, but my embarrassment grew even greater. To this day, I have never learned how to smoke.

The food-throwing antics that started in the Company cafeteria often carried over into Company social functions at local hotels and restaurants. Rarely was McCormick & Company allowed to return. After one large party at the old Southern Hotel on Light Street, the manager called after a week and said, "Okay, we give up, where is it?" Someone had hidden some Limburger cheese in a heating vent.

But not all the party antics were in town. During World War II, the Company purchased an island on Eastern Bay, off the Chesapeake Bay. While some experimental farming was done at "Parson Island," facilities there were used mostly for holding meetings and for customer duck hunting and fishing.

One year at the annual Sales Board meeting at Parson Island, C.P. took his boat down and, along with the regular island boat, transported the group ten miles down the Miles River to Longfellows Restaurant at St. Michaels. Before dinner, C.P. suggested that several people be thrown overboard. After a pushing frenzy ensued, everyone had been thrown over but C.P., who was directing traffic from on top of the cabin, and Bud Weiser, Vice President of Sales. Bud was leaving later that evening for New York and was attired in a handsome blue pinstripe suit. Amid terrible protest, Bud was eventually thrown overboard also. All this activity attracted a crowd of people, and one of them asked the owner of the restaurant what was going on. He said, "They're from McCormick & Company, and they're all crazy, and the craziest guy of all is the one on top of the boat directing all the action. That's Charlie McCormick."

The group eventually went into the restaurant dripping wet and, as usual, enjoyed their first and last dinner there.

But C.P. had a serious side too, and this carried over from McCormick business into other civic, educational, and sports interests. He served as Chairman of the Board of Regents at the

A typical ending of a sales board dinner during the 50s and 60s.

University of Maryland. He went to Geneva, Switzerland three times as the United States' Employer Delegate to the International Labor Organization. He was a member of the regional Federal Reserve Board and a number of other business organizations.

Having been branded a Communist by other Baltimore business executives in the 1930s for profit sharing and his liberal personnel policies, he took delight in assisting other companies who had heard about his Multiple Management philosophy. Many came to visit and see firsthand what had made McCormick so successful. The irony is that he detested Communism so much that he wrote extensively of the perils of it in his book on Multiple Management, called THE POWER OF PEOPLE.

There were many occasions where C.P. played a big role in the future of Baltimore sports. The first was as Chairman of the Board of the old Baltimore Colts in 1948. In 1947, a Washingtonian by

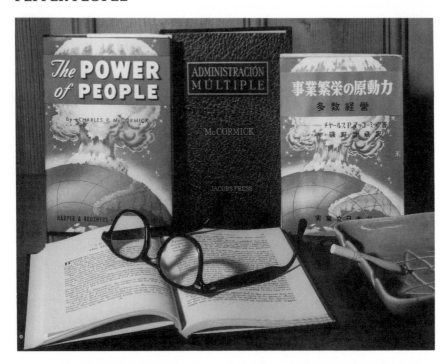

THE POWER OF PEOPLE BY C. P. was published in many languages around the world.

the name of Bob Rodenberg called C.P. and said that he and four of his friends in Washington had bought the Miami Seahawks. They explained the team had gone bankrupt, and they planned to move it to Baltimore to be a member of the All-American Football Conference. Charlie and his friend Jake Embry, Manager of WITH radio and President of the Baltimore Bullets championship basketball team, agreed to join Rodenberg with a few other small, local investors.

As the first season progressed, Rodenberg never communicated with the local investors, and when asked how the team was doing financially, his response was, "Oh, we're doing really well." However, when November came, according to Jake Embry, everyone found that the team was broke again. After a meeting was held with Mayor Tommy D'Alesandro and the league commissioner, an appeal went out to local business for financing. Local business put up $160,000, and $40,000 more of stock was sold in small units to the public. Jake was elected President and C.P. Chairman. The next year went very well. The team tied for the Eastern Division championship! A playoff game was played in Baltimore with Buffalo to see who would play the Cleveland Browns in the championship game.

A terribly controversial call was made by the referee late in that game when a Buffalo player caught a pass, turned around and ran ten yards, was hit, and fumbled, with the Colts recovering the ball. The referee called it an incomplete pass, and Buffalo then drove for the winning touchdown.

A riot ensued as people jumped out of the stands to get at the referee. Jake Embry was sitting with the football commissioner, who said, "Isn't that Zanvyl Kreiger down there trying to hit the referee?" (Zanvyl was a prominent attorney, and his family owned the prosperous Gunther Brewing Company. Zanvyl was also one of the local Colt owners.) Sure enough, it was Zanvyl, all five feet, two inches, jumping up and down out on the fringe of the crowd, swinging his fists and trying to hit the referee. The referee might have been killed if the players hadn't surrounded him and escorted him to the clubhouse. They later smuggled him onto the Buffalo bus to avoid the huge crowd that remained outside the dressing room to get him.

This defeat cost the Colts a lot of championship money. Coach Cecil Isbell, former quarterback for the Green Bay Packers, was directed to get out and buy, trade for, or draft any additional players that he needed to fill any holes that he felt he had. He assured the owners that he did not need to do any trading or buying; he was standing pat for the following season.

In 1949, the owner of a local transfer company who wanted to run the team took over. Although he had signed a letter agreeing not to profit personally from any team success, he sold the team the next year to the league. Despite having some great players, such as Y.A. Tittle, the team had won only two games. Y.A. Tittle went to San Francisco.

When C.P. was involved with the Colts, he put together a

group called the Colts Associates. He asked them to direct marketing and publicity activities and to originate half-time activities. John Conley, McCormick's Public Relations Manager and Assistant to the President, was involved in this and hosted some of the meetings at Light Street. Coaches Cecil Isbell and Walter Driskill and some of the players used to visit and sometimes stay for lunch in the "Crow's Nest," which was a small room off the boardroom.

Y.A. Tittle visited one day after the season. He announced that he had an off-season job selling "freight forwarding" and wanted to know "if we needed any."

Speaking of the Colts, we hired all-pro tackle Artie Donovan to do some promotional work for us on a new product called Fluffy mashed potatoes – a perfect match if I've ever seen one. I took him uptown to lunch at the old Merchants Club right before the training season. He declined food because he had to get his weight down. "You know . . . like if I eat food, then I can't drink beer; too many calories." So I ate lunch while Artie drank his.

After doing public appearances for us for a year promoting Fluffy, we had another meeting, at which time he told this story:

> **After we won the championship, sometime later I decided to invite the whole team over for a party. [Artie owned two liquor stores, and his wife ran their country club.] I decided to use the Fluffy potatoes and got a big barrel to mix them in. I put the Fluffy potatoes in the barrel, added many gallons of milk, and stirred the potatoes up with a baseball bat. Man, you know, those Fluffy potatoes really get hard! It was a hot day, and I'm stirring and sweating into the Fluffy potatoes. I stir and I sweat and I stir and I sweat! They never did get "fluffy."**

One never knows what goes on in the back of a kitchen . . . maybe that's a blessing!

The "Crow's Nest" I mentioned earlier was a room where C.P. occasionally invited a few guests for lunch. During World War II, it was decorated with paraphernalia sent back to C.P. by McCormick service personnel. Flags, pictures, paratrooper boots,

etc. completely covered the walls. Throughout the war, C.P. wrote letters to McCormick employees serving the military.

National personalities were often entertained in the Crow's Nest. One who attracted great attention one evening was Italian movie star Gina Lollobrigida, who was in town to publicize the National Heart Association Fund drive. C.P. was Chairman that year. She was gorgeous and nice, too.

PEPPER PEOPLE

After the Colts, another of C.P.'s sports ventures was as co-chairman of the stadium committee, charged with selection of a site and design of the new sports stadium. The other co-chairman was Glenn L. Martin, President of the famous Glenn L. Martin air-

VA-VA-VA-VOOM! One celebrity guest at Light Street building was Gina Lollobrigida.

craft company. Glenn Martin came up with a brilliant idea, which C.P. supported. Martin's idea was to build the first domed stadium in the history of football and baseball. Glenn and Charlie were almost laughed out of town for this "ridiculous idea," so the more conservative Memorial Stadium was built.

One lunch in the Crow's Nest initiated a discussion concerning out-of-stock items. C.P. remarked to Doc Badertscher that the sales department was complaining that we were out of insecticidal shampoo. Doc, who usually had a small piece of chewing tobacco in one cheek and a cigar stub in the other, was in charge of the insecticide department (manufacturing). Doc said not to worry, that he had a batch all mixed up "downstairs," but he couldn't bottle it yet because he hadn't tested it. He said he had to take a sample home and take a bath in it first!

This was early-on "Total Quality Management."

Doc Badertscher was given the responsibility for disposing of a batch of some very secret formula instant tea. He opened the tanks into the city's sewage system and promptly blew out all the manhole covers on Light Street. When the health inspectors came, our chief chemist innocently proclaimed, "It's not our tea!"

During one of the tougher business years, C.P. called the senior Board of Directors together and said he was afraid that the Company wasn't going to be able to fund all of the employees' vacations. He quietly announced a cutback in the salaries of the Board members in order to be able to assure all employees their vacations. As the year progressed, business brightened and the Board was given full salaries. By year end, things turned out quite well and additional bonuses were paid.

Here's a great story from C.P.'s wife, Anne, who served as one of the early Tea House hostesses, and then for many years as the "first lady" of the Company:

> **Charles was taken ill right at the time of our wedding and honeymoon. He had pneumonia with complications, which kept him home for a number of weeks. The day he finally was able to go to the plant, I was invited to join him for the general meeting of all employees in the cafeteria. When he was welcomed back, he told the employees how**

very happy he was to be back on the job, and then said, "I spent my whole honeymoon in bed." Everyone laughed, cheered, applauded, some even whistled. It took a long few seconds for him to realize their interpretation; then he introduced me, quite literally his "blushing bride."

Charles, as Anne always called him, always (and very rightly so) gave great credit to Anne for her valuable and loving support to him through his years of less than perfect health and the many traumas of building a small business into a larger one. Grow we did! Not only domestically, but internationally as well.

This growth led Ted Rodgers to be promoted in a rather interesting way. He was a clerk assisting the Director of International Sales and also assisted the Assistant Manager. The Director of Overseas Sales, Conrado De Lamar, and the assistant, Charlie Herdman, didn't get along. They argued; and when they argued, they did it in Spanish. All three men shared the same office, and one day there was a crash. When Ted turned around, there was Charlie Herdman on top of Conrado, beating the hell out of him. Both were rather large men, and Ted ran down the hall to get help. Finally separated, Conrado instructed Ted Rodgers to go to C.P.'s office and tell him what had happened. Ted wasn't happy about this, but orders were orders. C.P. laughed about it and asked Ted to send Herdman home after which he would talk to Lamar. Herdman was let go, and Ted Rodgers became the new Assistant Director. Eventually he became Managing Director of McCormick Overseas Trading Company.

Good salesmen come in all shapes, sizes, and personalities. One of the old-time, great pepper peddlers was Ed Crone, Regional Manager in Baltimore/Washington. During the Detroit introduction, I was sent out one day with Ed for further training. I'll never forget one call, which was to a medium-sized, independent grocer. The grocer was busy, but Ed made his pitch anyway. The grocer was shucking corn and putting it on display. He had one foot in a peach basket and was entirely surrounded by produce. Ed went through the entire McCormick "Baltimore Plan" sales pitch. When he finished and got no reaction, he started all over again. After hearing the pitch a third time, the grocer finally

"Honker" hi-jinks at Parson Island. Umpiring by Ed Crone.

reacted. He put down his corn, stopped Ed, and addressed me with a hearty laugh. He said, "Son, I've seen a lot of salesmen in my life, but this guy is *the best* I have ever seen!" Then he went back to husking his corn. Great compliment, but he never did give us an order!

During C.P.'s time, another of the great characters was Director of Purchasing Lester Jones. Lester was just about "king of the hill" in the spice industry because he represented McCormick, which was number one. He bought more pepper than anybody but the Soviet Union. In an era when "tippling" was more in vogue, Lester was no piker. He did his fair share at the American Spice Trade Association's (ASTA) functions, which were always held in a relaxed resort atmosphere.

Lester usually had so much fun playing "king" at the annual

convention that he often wouldn't eat the entire time; he drank. Late one evening at an ASTA affair, a very sober and proper English gentleman (but somewhat of a wise guy, too), whose firm was an important trader in black pepper, thought it would be fun to josh Lester a bit over his deepening state of inebriation. He kept intimating that Lester had only a limited understanding of the black pepper market. (Incidentally, black pepper represented about 40 percent of our profits in those days.) At the time, the price of pepper was about a dollar a pound.

The Englishman thought he'd have some fun with Lester by throwing him an offhanded offer of "50¢ delivered" in a smart-aleck flippant way. Thoroughly "tippled," Lester appeared to accept the offer enthusiastically, although with garbled gusto. "You got 200 tons at half a buck," said Lester. The Englishman was sure that Lester would forget the incident, and the evening continued.

The next morning at breakfast, out came a most nattily attired, sober, and somber Lester, who very properly and neatly sat himself down beside the Englishman. Then he asked, "Peter, did you bring your contract with you this morning for that 200 metric tons of Malabar black pepper at fifty cents per pound delivered in Baltimore? We'll choose the carrier!"

Lester's great friend and our major pepper supplier for many years was a delightful Dutchman by the name of Kurt Schussler. While attending an American Spice Trade Association ball at the old Hotel Astor on New York's Times Square, Kurt was attempting to return to his room one night after downing a large number of gin "silver bullets." A small crowd discovered Kurt standing in front of the tenth-floor broom closet, frantically pushing the door knob trying to get the down elevator.

Silver bullets apparently had a geographically disorienting effect on Kurt.

While having lunch at Thompson's Sea Girt House with McCormick Purchasing Director Howard Wolf, after three or four silver bullets, Kurt excused himself to go to the men's room. He took the wrong turn in the hall, opened the outside door to a section being remodeled, and fell one and a half stories down. Missed after half an hour, he was finally dragged back to the table, bloodied and bruised, by two waiters. What did he ask for? Another silver bullet.

Kurt's wife was probably the funniest lady I have ever met. She was a large woman, quite pretty, and looked like a giant baby doll. She could spit out a constant stream of one-liners and would laugh at them uproariously. One evening in New York, after a group of us had seen C.P. and Anne off to Europe on the Queen Elizabeth, about ten of us went to the Copacabana to take in the show. The Copa usually had good entertainment, but it was a scary place, run by the Mob. Big, mean-looking bouncers inspected you as you walked in. Not a nice feeling at all. Once you were inside, however, it was a great place.

We were having a delightful time, and Kurt's wife, Julia, was entertaining all of us as usual. Lester Jones' wife, Elsie, didn't tell the jokes, but she could laugh almost as loud as Julia. Whenever these two ladies got together, everybody laughed the entire evening.

Well, the entertainment at the Copa that evening wasn't too good. It was Ted Lewis, an old vaudevillian whose best days had passed. Lewis's jokes were so bad that Julia started telling funnier ones of her own at our table. The noise got to Ted Lewis, and he stopped in the middle of his show. After some moments of silence, he looked at our table and asked, "Am I going to do the entertaining here, or are you?" With that, Elsie Jones shouted, "We are!"

Within seconds, four big, mean-looking, tuxedoed thugs surrounded our table and said, "Out!" They escorted us right out into the street. It was perfect. We missed a terrible show and avoided paying a big bill.

While C.P. liked to listen to different views and draw a consensus, he didn't lose many battles when he felt strongly about something.

One time, however, he did lose. The Corporate Board went out to Hunt Valley one cold and windy afternoon to pick out the spot for the new plant for the Grocery Products Division. We stood on a part of Route 83, where C.P. proclaimed we should build the new plant so that it could be seen as all the world traveled by. "No," said the financial people, "that piece is too valuable to use for our own plant. We are in the land development business now, and we must think of how to get the best value for our property." I've never seen C.P. more upset, but in the end he succumbed.

C.P. was not what you would call a polished speaker, but he was an interesting one because he always had something positive to say and to sell. One evening, he was speaking at an outside banquet, and in his introductory remarks he proudly said, "I am the father of four children." A voice from the back of the room asked, "Mr. McCormick, do you have any other hobbies?"

Another evening, at an association meeting where C.P. was the featured speaker, the meeting droned on until past ten o'clock. He was finally introduced. He stood up, tore up his notes, and said to the crowd, "It's too late, let's go home." He received a standing ovation.

But everyday life at McCormick was not a standing ovation. During one very tough year, C.P. called the Board of Directors together and said to them, "Things are really rough right now, and it is necessary that we sell one million dollars' worth of insect powder immediately." Everyone was dispatched to the South and within ten days reached the sales objective. Six months later, DDT came on the market, which made the old formula obsolete. So all the merchandise was shipped back to the plant, where it was reformulated and repackaged.

In the Fall issue of the 1963 *Tea Time Tales*, C.P. wrote an article called "The Future is Bright." This article clearly presents C.P.'s business philosophy:

> In commenting on the last chapter of THE POWER OF PEOPLE [C.P.'s book on McCormick management], may I take the liberty of writing as an elder to a youngster entering business in the house of McCormick, observing the "Multiple Management" formula for human relationships. This chapter, written some 31 years ago, was titled "The Future is Bright." Today the caption is still appropriate. In fact, our future today is even "brighter."
>
> The pattern of the average youngster in business is

eagerness to learn and to succeed, with a desire to prove to others his superior talents. Often in so doing, he becomes too selfish in his forcefulness and does not accomplish as much as he would if he had taken time out to study himself analytically. To do so one needs advisors, instructors that are considerate, and trainers that are already skillful. This takes a team of different talents. The Board system can be a great asset in sponsoring each youth into areas of his greatest potentiality. Only through team play can he learn the art of management quickly. He can learn to observe first before criticizing. He can test his views in speech and through reason, not in misspent energy or action. He learns to be unselfish and think of the whole organization – not of his own troubles and success alone.

So, in building himself and learning about himself he can save years of valuable time. He also learns that a stern administrator need not be cold-hearted and that a flattering friend is often a pitfall. From these Boards he can educate himself for positions of high responsibility and for serving on higher administrative boards. Multiple Management is a kindly disciplinary force which encourages growth of character and the development and perfection of new ideas. Like the Constitution of the United States, it does not force anyone to do anything, but if the rules are followed, everyone benefits for having lived under its precepts.

The future is actually brighter than 25, 50, or 100 years ago. The possibilities of the future, in the vastness of the atomic and scientific space age, are unlimited. It is true that our life today is dangerous; but have we ever lived in an age free of danger of wars, famines, revolutions or social upheavals?

We have great problems today – delinquency of youth, Communism, radicalism, etc. So what? Our forefathers had the threat of Indian arrows, wars, slaughters, bodily harm ever over their heads. Yet they carved a "Great Nation" for us out of the wilderness of fear and fright. We cannot *yearn* for these things, we must *earn* them.

Don't duck your business responsibility or your civic duty. Never be arrogant! Learn to defeat by good judgment and a just tongue. Scrap or disagree if you have to, but always fairly and decently. In other words, be a good citizen in all phases of life – business, home, and community.

So, to youth, my final advice for maintaining the best business is to go the Multiple Management route. Follow it carefully, improve it openly with your partners. Be a full partner, not a "party" man. Learn to develop a habit of liking people, studying them so you can judge them better in your relations, since this knowledge is needed to lead others after you have learned to be a good follower.

The Future is Bright! Forget the negative side, pass up the pessimistic things and look *upwards* and be happy that you were born an American – free! Try to achieve and make something of your life. Learn finally to give more than you get! I believe happiness and success are yours for the taking.

This can best be learned through our Multiple Management system. Good Luck!

C. P. (seated, center) surrounded by the core management team: (l-r standing): Walter Davis, "Doc" Badertscher, Jim Welsh, Lester Jones, Brooke Furr. (l-r seated): Conrado De Lamar, Leonard Fardwell, John Curlett, George Armour, C. P., Grayson Luttrell, Norm Settle, Fred Ensey, Paul Frisch.

PEPPER PEOPLE

Although Charlie's primary business focus and the legend that he left was his "people focus," he did have one major financial goal for the Company. That was to achieve one hundred million dollars in sales volume. It happened in 1969, the year that he retired from the Company and was elected Chairman Emeritus.

The last time that I saw him was in June of 1970, just before his life ended. I was running for the train station, briefcase in hand, when a horn blew, and I turned to see a waving, smiling father. What a way to remember a winner.

Chapter Four

Schilling

In 1947, the world's largest spice and extract company acquired the second-largest. It was a perfect acquisition, because McCormick was number one in the East and Schilling number one in the West, with very little overlap in sales territories. Although in hindsight the acquisition was one of the most important moves in the Company's history, it took lots of courage at the time, since McCormick was only slightly larger than Schilling.

In fact, the Baltimore banks would not lend McCormick the money for the acquisition. Finally, the local consortium agreed to finance the deal on the condition that they would then *own* a piece of McCormick. That blew any possibility of local cooperation. Over the Board of Directors' dead bodies would some Baltimore financial institution own McCormick & Company!

It was billed to the industry as a merger, which was a great description, because for many years later the insiders were still asking who bought whom. The rivalry between McCormick and the Schilling Division remained intense even after we were united. McCormick people thought that Schilling should succumb to the parent's policies, but the boys from the West only wanted to outperform their Eastern cousins. From a sales growth standpoint, they usually did. From a productivity standpoint, they didn't. They had to cope with work rules and attitudes sponsored courtesy of Harry Bridges' Longshoremen's Union in San Francisco.

Schilling's President was a tough old ex-H.J. Heinz sales manager by the name of C.E. (Clarence) Miller. John Curlett, then

*As these old packages show, the Schilling name had quite
a history long before McCormick purchased the West Coast
Company in 1947.*

Executive Vice President of McCormick, was appointed as liaison
officer with the Schilling Division. In those days, there were no
jets to the West Coast, and flight times were so long that trains
were regularly used. John spent a lot of time traveling to the West
and most of his time there armwrestling with C.E., who had two
reactions to all corporate desires. The first was to fight; the second was to agree reluctantly. This latter mode, however, only
lasted until John boarded the train back to Baltimore, when all
that was agreed to was forgotten.

The Schilling name was even more powerful than McCormick,
with higher per capita sales in its territories. I've always claimed
that anyone who suggests changing the Schilling brand name to
McCormick has obviously never been west of the Mississippi River.

McCormick's Vice President-Sales was Bernard (Bud) Weiser. Bud used to get excellent seating in fancy New York restaurants by calling and introducing himself as Mr. Bud Weiser. The maitre d' would invariably react very excitedly and say, "Oh yes, Mr. Budweiser, we'll have a wonderful table for you."

Bud and his marketing troops came up with a very successful sales plan called "The Baltimore Plan." This was the original plan that transformed product, price, and quality selling of spices one at a time into programmed selling of the entire line. The Baltimore Plan was a "profit" story to the grocer, offering our expertise in merchandising, item selection, promotion, etc., with each spice department tailored to that specific store, its ethnic neighborhood, and its geographical needs.

We put in floor stands or metal shelf equipment to display a complete line, ordered out the merchandise, put it on the shelf,

C. E. Miller, President of Schilling.

priced it, rotated it, and promoted it seasonally. We eliminated all backroom stocks.

It was a very successful innovation – real leadership. Meanwhile, Schilling was still slugging it out the old-fashioned way, product by product, and also doing *that* very successfully.

Bud Weiser preached that the grocery business was changing rapidly. With the advent of the supermarket, good marketers should now realize that 20 percent of the stores do 80 percent of the business. You could only afford to call on those 20 percent stores. He tried and tried to convince Schilling's C.E. that this was the way to go.

In December of 1950, between Christmas and New Year's, I joined John Curlett on the train trip west for the annual two-day

"The Baltimore Plan," a marketing technique, was developed in the late 1940s by McCormick to provide customers with a complete line of spice products.

The Schilling Headquarters at 2nd and Folsom was a San Francisco landmark for many years.

Schilling sales meeting. We had recently had a sales meeting in Baltimore where everyone was wearing "20% of the stores do 80% of the business" buttons.

Well, we arrived at the old Schilling plant at 2nd and Folsom Streets in San Francisco, where C.E. Miller was standing outside the front door greeting all the visitors. With a grin from ear to ear, he presented us each with a *huge, orange* button which contained the theme of *his* meeting: "100% of the stores do 100% of the business!" One-upped by Schilling again.

One of the things C.E. did at that sales meeting was to show a competitive product test. Schilling had a very high oil content in their lemon extract, so they wanted to use the lemon extract as their quality comparison. (Schilling quality, on all products, was excellent.) At the coffee break, I said, "C.E., I bet you used to really tear us up with that lemon test." He smiled and said, "Well,

R. C. Crampton headed Schilling operations on the West Coast for many years.

young man, you know you guys really were pretty tough competitors," and gave me a big wink.

Before the annual sales meeting one year, C.E. told his Sales Manager, R.C. (Bob) Crampton, not to worry about the agenda because he had taken care of all of it. He said all Crampton had to do was be there. The meeting was started by C.E. in his usual fashion, which was to have a real attention-getter to start the agenda. As his attention-getter for many years, he would single out one person from the sales organization who he felt had not done a good job and publicly fire him at the meeting. On this day he took fifteen or twenty minutes to accomplish this and then said, "Bob, come on up and take over. It's your meeting!" Bob could have killed him.

Old C.E. had a way to handle outsiders too. A delegation came in to request that Schilling make available a junior executive to help with the San Francisco United Fund. They asked C.E. to lend them a manager for the period of one year. C.E.'s response was, "If I had someone like that I'd fire the S.O.B."

He was even tougher on a young investment counselor who called on him. C.E. asked the lad how rich he was. The answer was that the young man was just starting a family and had not had sufficient time to create any wealth. C.E. said, "Well, you come back to see me when you've made more money than I have; then maybe I'll let you tell me how to spend mine."

One of the most creative people I've ever met was McCormick's Advertising Director, Gerry Baxter. He also knew how to create controversy. Gerry eventually ended up as a top executive with J. Walter Thompson, the huge ad agency. Once Gerry accompanied Bud Weiser on a trip out West. While they were there, C.E. Miller took quite ill with an upset stomach. They were all in Los Angeles. C.E. was confined to his hotel room when Gerry visited late in the afternoon bringing him a present because he was sick. The present was a bag of peanuts for his upset stomach!

This is the same Gerry Baxter who attended a social function at C.P.'s house one evening. The guest of honor was a young Englishman whose first name was Peter. He was related to an important British friend of the Company. Gerry eventually grew tired of seeing this young man getting so much attention from our group and invited him into the laundry room for a private discussion. Since I reported to Baxter at the time, he invited me in also. I thought that Gerry was going to say something nice or give the young man some advice. However, Gerry launched into a tirade, telling the young guest what a dumb *&#@! he was, and that he didn't like him at all. Wow, I thought, this is rather bizarre – a young man from England is invited as a guest of honor by people he doesn't know, is placed on a pinnacle by new friends, and then suddenly finds himself in a laundry room being chewed out by someone he's never seen in his life. Peter was speechless and flabbergasted. I was speechless and flabbergasted.

When Gerry left the house that evening, he got in his car, which was parked right in front, made a "U" turn on the narrow street, and drove across the lawn of our former Vice President, George Armour, who lived right across the street. Since it was wintertime, the lawn was quite soggy, and the tire tracks remained as a remembrance of Gerry to both Mr. Armour and to C.P. for quite some time.

Gerry Baxter was also famous for his unexpected handling of Dr. Flory, our RH&R psychologist. When it was Baxter's turn to be "Flory-scoped," he listened patiently to the list of his short-comings until the end. Then he shook his finger in Dr. Flory's face and said, "Doctor, now let *me* tell *you* a thing or two," and launched into an explicit rebuttal.

Well, Doc never said he could win them all!

Jack Caffey, a regional sales manager at Schilling who went on to become General Manager of the International Division, recalls Thanksgiving of 1949, when C.E. Miller had reluctantly agreed with John Curlett to follow the McCormick tradition and distribute turkeys to all employees, even those under union contract (but not the salesmen, because "they'd probably buy whiskey with the allowance anyway.") The turkeys arrived on Wednesday, fresh and undressed (cheaper that way). Caffey claimed that his bird, with head, feet, innards, and pinfeathers still in place, was still quivering when he got it home.

C.E. got his revenge with John Curlett the next summer during the Schilling strike, when he said, "I knew we shouldn't have given those #!!@!! union employees those #!!@!! turkeys last year."

C.E. Miller's needling of Bud Weiser never ceased. This letter to Bud's Sales Manager Walter Driskill is priceless. (Walter eventually started the Dribeck Company and successfully introduced Beck's beer to the entire United States.)

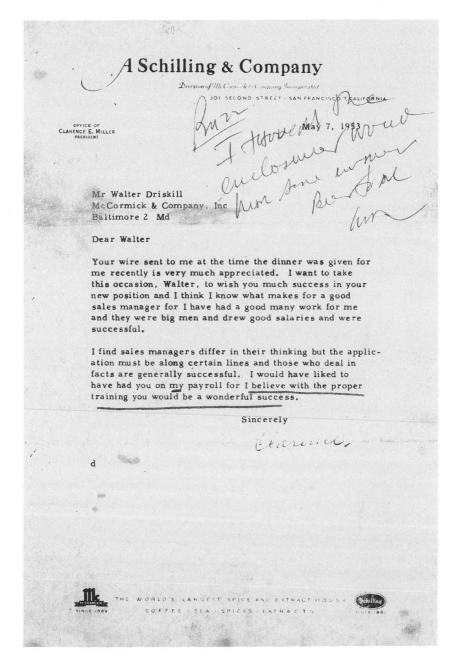

A Schilling & Company

Division of McCormick & Company Incorporated

301 SECOND STREET · SAN FRANCISCO 7, CALIFORNIA

OFFICE OF
CLARENCE E. MILLER
PRESIDENT

May 7, 1953

Mr Walter Driskill
McCormick & Company, Inc
Baltimore 2 Md

Dear Walter

Your wire sent to me at the time the dinner was given for
me recently is very much appreciated. I want to take
this occasion, Walter, to wish you much success in your
new position and I think I know what makes for a good
sales manager for I have had a good many work for me
and they were big men and drew good salaries and were
successful.

I find sales managers differ in their thinking but the applic-
ation must be along certain lines and those who deal in
facts are generally successful. I would have liked to
have had you on my payroll for I believe with the proper
training you would be a wonderful success.

Sincerely

Clarence

d

THE WORLD'S LARGEST SPICE AND EXTRACT HOUSE
COFFEE · TEA · SPICES · EXTRACTS
SINCE 1889   SINCE 1881

Letter to Driskill.

Eventually, C.E. retired, and for a short time, a triumvirate ran the division: Bob Crampton; C.E.'s son, John, who was Production Manager; and Walter Emmerling, the former President of the Ben Hur Spice Company. Ben Hur, a former competitor in Los Angeles, had been acquired by McCormick in 1953.

Bob Crampton was eventually elected General Manager, and he was a great one. One thing didn't change, however. He still wanted to beat the hell out of his East Coast cousins. He was the most competitive man I've ever met. He was always competing either by selling, negotiating, or playing golf, gin rummy, or liar's poker – whatever was the most timely. He never relaxed and always stayed totally focused. The Schilling guys all claimed they needed a raise just to be able to afford Crampton's winning ways. Everything was a bet.

He sent Trade Relations Director Clark Barrett into a fury once while entertaining him on the exclusive Cypress Point Golf Course in Monterey. When they arrived at the famous 200-yard, par three hole, at which you have to hit over the ocean into a sea breeze, Crampton said, "Clarkie, the way we play here is to go for it on your first attempt. If you go into the ocean, then play your second ball up the side rather than putting another ball in the ocean."

Clark hit his ball 220 yards into the wind, landing it right on the green. Crampton fell short into the Pacific Ocean. Crampton hit his second ball up the left-hand fairway, then chipped on and putted in for what would logically be a five. Clark parred the hole with a three. Crampton said, "Nice par, Clark." Clark said, "Thanks; what did you take?" Crampton said, "Par." Clark exploded, "What do you mean – you hit one in the ocean!" Crampton said, "I told you the rule: the first shot doesn't count." Clark yelled, "You #!!@!! West Coast hustler!" And he called him that for the rest of his life.

Crampton also got to Carter Parkinson on the golf course. Carter was General Manager of the McCormick Division when he bought a small farm on the Maryland/Pennsylvania line. The farm had seventy or eighty acres, and Carter loved it. Carter already had a big ego, and the farm only added to it. He talked about it incessantly.

One night after a sales meeting in Palm Springs, we went to a restaurant. I timed Carter. From the time we arrived at the restaurant until we finally left was a total of two and a half hours. During all that time, Carter talked about his farm. None of the other seven or eight of us at the table ever spoke, except briefly to order dinner.

Crampton was so tired of hearing about Carter's farm that he invited Carter to play golf at the Olympic Club in San Francisco. He matched Carter up with another guest, whom he had invited for a purpose. Bob introduced the guest to Carter as a customer. On the first tee, in conversation Crampton prompted Carter to tell the guy about his big farm in Maryland. For eighteen holes, Carter regaled the guy with stories about "his" pigs, "his" corn, "his" alfalfa, and so on.

After the game, in the clubhouse bar, Carter finally got around to asking Crampton's friend about *his* business. The guy in question was a major supplier of onion and garlic to our subsidiary, Gilroy Foods! So he told Carter he wasn't a *big* farmer, as California farmers go, but he had about 15,000 acres of onion and garlic in the Valley, another 5,000 acres down near Fresno, and several thousand acres in Texas. He also told Carter that he was running experimental crops on several thousand acres in Africa for the government. The project was to determine what crops are best for feeding the starving people of the world.

After Crampton came East and told this story to C.P., John Curlett and Ernie Issel, our Treasurer, the farm talk slowed a little.

Not many people ever got the best of Bob Crampton. But there are two times that I do remember:

At a general meeting, Bob presented a President's Award (now called the C.P. McCormick Award) to a plant worker. Bob was smiling broadly and said, "What would you like to say?" With all seriousness, the awardee said, "It's about time!" and sat down. For once, Crampton had nothing to say!

The other time was Clark Barrett's revenge for being hustled out of money over the golf hole at Cypress Point.

The Federal Trade Commission received a complaint from a competitor that Crampton had made a degrading remark about this competitor to a customer. While this was a very serious allegation, Clark Barrett and the guys back East thought it was hilarious that Crampton had been caught. Clark sent Crampton a postcard with a big, open-mouthed hippopotamus on it. The hippo's words were: "Big mouth!"

Ed Ellis was a tea salesman extraordinaire, Junior Board Chairman and later Vice President, Sales and Marketing, Schilling Division.

Well, Crampton completely lost it. He immediately called up John Curlett, who was by then President, described the hippo card, and told him how this was definitely not funny. Later, John called Clark in and told him that the card had almost caused the start of World War III.

Crampton probably did start another minor war of his own, although we never heard the end of the story, I'm sure.

Once Crampton was visited in his office by an Internal Revenue agent who wanted to ask some questions about the expenses claimed on his return. The agent was a large, unattractive woman. During the course of the conversation, she remarked that she couldn't believe that a restaurant bill could be as large as one that Crampton had declared. Crampton claims he said to her, "I guess you can't. You've probably never been to as nice a restaurant as that." To the day of his fatal heart attack, R.C. Crampton was always on the offensive.

McCormick has been fortunate over the years in having only a limited number of personal disasters. One of these happened far out over the Pacific Ocean to Ed Ellis, whose plane went down on a business trip to Hawaii. Originally from the East, for some years Ed had been in charge of tea sales for the Company and was an inspirational leader.

On one trip to the Midwest, where McCormick tea had never been sold or even heard of, Ed sold seventeen consecutive, new retail accounts. One of his famous rebuttals to the typical turndown of "I never get any calls for it" was, "I bet you've never gotten a call for a haircut either; but if you put a barber chair in your store, you'd get a lot of haircut business."

When Ed was lost, he had been responsible for Schilling sales and marketing. He was replaced in this position by Wayne Dellinger.

Joe Harper recalls that Dellinger was a master at developing, motivating, and perpetuating the image that sales people can make – and for that matter, *is* the difference – in making something happen inside a grocery store. Dellinger constantly challenged people and didn't hesitate to chastise those who "weren't prepared to take advantage of opportunities whenever they might appear." When everything was running smoothly, he began to worry that things were too easy and, therefore, "competition was bound to take advantage of us."

Dellinger was great fun to kid and tease. He was a gentleman and usually professed not to understand what you were needling him about; then the curves of his mouth would break into the beginning of a big wide grin. He was Crampton's biggest "turkey" because of their close relationship. Crampton just loved to take Dellinger's money away from him. If it didn't work on the golf course, they would rush to the gin rummy table. If Crampton didn't win there, it would go on to liar's poker.

Dellinger was an early-to-bed guy but never liked to admit it. He would always suggest places for the group to go after dinner, and then sneak off to bed so he could be fresher than anyone in the morning. He got caught in the act on numerous occasions.

He tells this story on himself:

> We were having a dinner meeting one evening in San Francisco with our regional sales managers at one of our fine restaurants. There were about twenty of us at the table.
>
> Bob Crampton said to one of the fellows sitting three or four places from me, "I will bet you $10 I know what Dellinger will eat for dinner." The fellow answered by saying, "I call your bet." Bob then said, "He will order a New York cut steak." Dellinger heard the conversation as he was about to order the New York cut steak. He then gave the waiter an order for veal cutlets. The next day Bob came into Dellinger's office and asked for a $20 bill until he cashed a check. A week or so later, Dellinger reminded him that he had not returned the $20. Crampton said, "It will just cost you that for double-crossing me." End of $20. End of story.

The hardest I ever saw Wayne Dellinger laugh was one day at the Olympic Club. He was a pretty good golfer, and I was a hacker. I swung a three wood on a fairway shot and hit about six inches behind the ball. A huge clod of dirt went farther than the ball, and my right arm felt like an elephant had fallen on it. Normally

Wayne Dellinger was Vice-President, Sales and Marketing,
Schilling Division.

the complete gentleman, Dellinger doubled up in laughter, which
didn't subside for the next two holes.

Jack Sassard, who eventually became General Manager of the
Schilling Division, went West to supervise advertising and promotion for Schilling. Jack came from McCormick, where he had
been in charge of tea sales. Despite all the great tea hustlers we

Jack Sassard transferred west and later became General Manager, Schilling Divsion.

sent to Schilling, we still were never successful in selling that product out West.

Jack is still laughing about Dellinger's experience in C.P.'s summer home, called OP HONK, on the Severn River near Annapolis, Maryland. Dellinger, Sassard, Crampton, and Ron Irwin, Schilling's Director of Sales, were being entertained by C.P. and Anne. Now, you have to know that Wayne Dellinger is a fastidious person, always looking like he walked out of a fashion ad.

It was dessert time, and C.P. picked up a can of Reddi Whip to decorate his dessert. Never mechanically inclined, C.P. had the Reddi Whip turned in the wrong direction and splattered Dellinger completely. It couldn't have happened to a better victim.

That may have been one of the reasons Dellinger absolutely hated to travel East.

Dellinger and Ron Irwin were a strong team, and Ron moved up to Vice President-Marketing and Sales when Dellinger retired. Ron used to say of R.C. Crampton, "R.C. won't be happy until he has every penny's worth of spice business west of the Mississippi River."

Ron's sales meetings were fun, particularly the sales dinners. He always had a gag gift for everyone in the room.

For three years, when I was still a pretty young guy, I was the liaison officer with the Schilling Division. When I attended the management Christmas party at the elegant Fairmont Hotel in San Francisco, I knew I would be called on for a few words. Having constantly been accused by my parents of being a person of "few words," and rightly so, I have always had to give some thought ahead of time if I knew I would be called on to speak.

Crampton started the evening by saying, "We've just had a great year." He paused and looked at the crowd and said, "Now that we got that over with, we can talk about the new year." Shortly after that, he called on me. I responded with a few well-chosen words and then relaxed for the evening.

After Crampton had called on everyone in the room, it still wasn't that late, so he called on me again. This time, I was relaxed, completely off guard, and *blank*. So I said the same thing again. I don't think many people noticed, but it was an excellent lesson in always being prepared . . . with at least one more story.

The Schilling regional sales meetings were always a good experience, hard work but upbeat. They definitely always had the atmosphere of a gathering of winners. The social times are most memorable, particularly one meeting held at the Casa Munras Hotel in Monterey, California.

The first evening of that meeting ended with the entire group arguing with the management of the hotel. They were trying to get me reinstated into the lounge. At the egging of my Schilling friends, I had tried to play the drums while the trio was on break. Twice during the evening, I was asked to stop; but knowing that I had played the drums a little as a kid, the others encouraged me at every break to return to the bandstand. The third time, I was ushered out onto the street, followed by the entire Schilling group. After some of the absolutely greatest salesmanship I have ever heard in my life, we were allowed to re-enter the hotel lounge . . . provided I didn't get near the drums.

The next evening, before dinner, was the completion of the gin rummy contest. One of the finalists was Jerry Reiland, nicknamed the "preacher" because of his emotional speaking style. Jerry, the Denver Regional Manager, was quite excited to be in the finals. With all of us standing around watching the finale, Jerry nervously sipped his drinks until he started knocking them over. Then the group would move the contestants to a new table and refresh the drinks.

It developed into quite an animated game, since every time Jerry's opponent ginned, Jerry would leap up like he had been hit by a machine gun, yell, "Ahhh," and turn over the drink and the table. Finally, he lost.

At dinner, we sat next to each other. The first course was soup, served in big tureens. We all watched as Jerry slowly slumped forward, face first into the middle of his minestrone. Jerry was sound asleep as we carried him past the maitre d' on the way to his room. We were greeted with a slightly bent smile.

Los Angeles grew to become the largest McCormick & Company market. Two of the men who contributed much to the building of that market were John Wertzberger and Cecil Haynes.

John was a sincere, hardworking sales supervisor, while Cecil was a character. Originally from Tennessee, Cecil was always laughing and never appeared ruffled. He was famous for one thing: he loved to have the "brass" come and visit his customers with him. Cecil always laughed his way through the meeting. However, when the conversation inevitably turned serious and the customer asked a tough question or made a complaint, Cecil would stare at the ceiling and act as if he wasn't even part of the meeting. The poor visiting executive, who probably didn't understand the details of the problem, was left to fend for himself.

Crampton knew sales talent when he saw it and asked Jack Loomis to join the Company. Jack had worked at Spice Islands and was very well liked by the trade. He became known as "Loomie," which later became "Loomie Baby."

Loomie was running one of his first sales meetings in L.A. and putting some of the newer salesmen through some role playing. One person was playing the salesman and another the customer. Loomie asked the newest sales apprentice how he would respond to his first call if the grocer said, "The last Schilling salesman was so terrible I will never buy from your company again, and I am throwing the entire Schilling line out." Loomie repeated, "What would be your response?" The new lad said, "I would ask him where his telephone is." Loomie said, "Why?" He said, "Because then I'd call the Schilling office and ask for Mr. Loomis. When he came on the line, I'd say, 'Loomie Baby, you've got a problem!' " I believe that's how Loomie got his nickname.

The morning after one particularly long and tough night at a supermarket convention, Loomie came into the hotel suite and poured himself another big one, the same stuff he had been drinking the night before. With that, he turned around and announced to all that "Loomie Baby is going to have a BIG hangover – but not today!"

One year, the Company had some major changes in its pension plan, and this subject was on the agenda for all regional sales meetings. Gordon Yates, Human Relations Manager for Schilling who later became Corporate Vice President - Administration, was asked to make the presentation at the Minneapolis meeting.

Gordon joined Schilling executives for the flight from San Francisco to Denver, where they all had connecting flights. Gordon, who didn't travel all the time like the salesmen, was concerned about getting aboard his connecting flight, but they assured him that he had plenty of time. They kept insisting that he remain with them in the airport bar. When he finally took his leave, he found out too late that his flight was at the extreme opposite end of the terminal. The gate was closed when he arrived. Being late was unheard of to a former military man like Gordon!

Since that was the last flight of the day to Minneapolis, Gordon spent the night on a bench in the terminal. He got on an early flight the next morning, and arrived at the hotel just in time to make his presentation. After a few introductory remarks, blasting Ron Irwin and friends for making him miss his flight, he got down to the complex agenda for the day. He looked down at his notes . . . and he looked . . . and he looked. Finally, looked up and said, "I am afraid that my eyes won't focus." He was excused and sent up to his room for some sleep. He came back later to make his presentation, but he never trusted sales guys again.

While all this action was going on, a young engineer from Baltimore by the name of Harry Wells was sent out West in charge of Schilling manufacturing, with no idea that one day he would become CEO of the entire Company. When Harry became General Manager of the Schilling Division, Don Jeter replaced him as Schilling's Director of Manufacturing. Jeter tells this strange San Francisco tale:

> Back in 1966 in the old Schilling building in San Francisco, a "ghost" began haunting the place late in the year. Coming to work in the morning, we began to notice things were in different places in the offices at times. Food was missing from the cafeteria. We brought in the burglar alarm people and added a sound detection system in the office area, hoping to pick up signs of an intruder. The alarms were not tripped, but things continued to be moved about and to disappear. The janitors were put under surveillance, with no results. In February 1966, the odd occur-

Harry Wells began his career as a summer employee while studying engineering at the University of Maryland.

rences suddenly stopped, only to start up again several months later. One Monday morning, there were dusty footprints across the floor in the bottle filling area. No one claimed ownership. We called in the police. They came by, took down information, and said they would put the building under a watch for intruders. No improvement occurred.

One morning several weeks later, a meeting was being held in General Manager Bob Crampton's office, when a thump was heard above the false ceiling in his office. Then a grunt, and a leg came crashing through the ceiling, followed by a curse. The leg then pulled back up, and a commotion was heard above the ceiling. Everyone rushed out of the room and headed for the second floor and the door that opened into the open space above all of the first floor offices.

There were no lights, so maintenance was called to bring some up. Lights soon arrived, and a few brave people entered the area. There were a few beams in place to walk on. After a close, careful look, no one was found. However, a "nest" was discovered in a corner. It contained plant uniforms, caps, blankets, food, and other clothing. We now knew someone was living up there and apparently had been doing so for some months. We called the police, who staked out the building, brought in dogs, and searched the building. No one was found. However, the disappearing food and movement of items stopped – at least for awhile.

A few months later, things again began to disappear. The "nest" in the ceiling area was observed; nothing was there. The next weekend, the sonic alarm went off, and police with dogs were dispatched to the plant. They gained entry and the dogs soon found the "phantom." His name was Peter Pain, a local down-and-outer. He had gained access by jumping down onto the coffee-area roof from a freeway approach and had found an open window in the upper coffee-grinding room. He later rigged an old, unused fire escape to go to and from the roof from the street. When it got cold (40 degrees in San Francisco), he just moved into the building, got a uniform, and on occasion even had meals in the cafeteria on second shift. We had recently hired a number of new people on that shift, so everyone thought he belonged. He had left the building after the ceiling episode, but returned shortly and planned to be more careful. He was put in jail for a few days, and we had the window secured (or thought we did).

All went well for a month or so, when we again began to notice small things. A few random footprints in the morning after clean up. Things missing, food missing. We knew Peter had been released from jail, so we called the police again. They made several "raids" with dogs and finally caught the intruder. Sure enough, it was Peter again. By now he had become an established name for anything that went wrong in the building – "Peter was here." He went to jail again. We checked the window where he had gained access before and noted he had somehow removed the hinges to enter the building. We then bolted the window shut and removed the unused fire escape. We never heard from Peter again, even though we told him to come back and apply for a job when he got out of jail. Apparently, he liked the freedom to roam around, but didn't want to work and be forced to follow rules.

Another unusual story came from sales executive Joe Wertzberger, who tells this Indian tale:

One of the better quick liners I ever heard was delivered by an American Indian consumer of ours in Gallup, New Mexico. About twenty years ago, I was sent there to help with a store remodeling project. Early on I quickly learned that the state had recently forbidden the sale of alcoholic beverages (firewater) to the Indian population. Consequently, according to a store manager I was talking to, the sale of certain of our extracts was absolutely exploding. That's right, the Indians were thought to be substituting vanilla extract for Jim Beam. This store manager told me to just wait and at some point during the course of my day, I would see what he was talking about. Furthermore, it was his responsibility to help prevent the menace of drunken Indians in his community. He had to screen the intentions of some Indians before they bought our extracts.

Soon enough, a big, hulking, unshaven old Indian came staggering up the baking aisle wearing a dirty, wide-brimmed black hat. He didn't have a leg under him. It was obvious that if his given name was actually "Running Deer," he could have easily passed for "Vanilla Breath." I was busy tearing apart our department. He briefly stopped next to me and immediately reached up with this enormous paw of a hand of his and snatched up three bottles of 8-ounce vanilla extract. As he swayed back down the aisle in the direction of the checkout stands, I decided to follow him and watch the screening process take place.

The store manager looked at him, then glanced at me, then back to him and rather suspiciously, but firmly, asked, "What are you goin' to do with all that vanilla?" Without missing a beat, that ol' Indian looked up at him stoically, stared him straight in the eyes, and said, "Squaw gonna make big cake." It was priceless.

In earlier days, shortly after the Schilling acquisition, several of our Eastern advertising agency executives went out to visit the Schilling plant. We received a call from them on the morning of their first trip to California. With great excitement, they told us when they arrived at the Schilling plant, there was a gun battle going on in the warehouse. Following an argument, one of the employees went out to his automobile, grabbed his revolver, and returned to the warehouse to chase and shoot at his fellow worker. These advertising executives were really impressed with their first real look at the "Wild West." They always had a somewhat distorted view of California living.

Chapter Five

Sales, Sales, and More Sales – Up, Up, and Away

McCormick Sales Manager Tim Harris was working with a newly promoted regional manager in New England. They were making a series of business reviews in customer offices and were visiting a large customer in the area. The meeting was held in the President's office, with three of his executives in attendance. They were all old friends of Tim's. After the usual small talk, the regional manager distributed copies of the sales review and began to discuss the contents. The President interrupted with a question: Why was the amount for advertising funds much higher than the amount of the check he had received a few days earlier? The regional manager immediately began to do a softshoe routine about gross sales versus net sales and how some items may not qualify for advertising, etc. The President was very complimentary about the volume of business he was doing with us. He had not realized how large his spice business had gotten.

While all of this was going on, Tim was scanning the report. He noticed that the name of the customer listed at the top of the page was not the account being visited, but its major competitor and our number one customer in the area. He did not want to call the error to the attention of the others and reveal confidential information to a competitor. On instinct, he stood up and announced that this was another case of computer miscalculations, and that when he got back to the office there was going to be a serious meeting on getting reports accurately produced.

The regional manager thought Tim was losing his mind when

he reached over the President's desk and picked up the report and put it into his own briefcase. Tim continued to act irate as he took copies out of the hands of the executives, while he apologized for the errors and promised to return with the right information. Tim said a *very serious* discussion was held in the regional manager's car after leaving that customer's parking lot!

When Dave Michels was Vice President of Sales, he spent one day with Earl Thompson, New York Regional Manager. Earl was to drive Dave out to see the President of Hill's Supermarket. The Company had just begun to make presentations to Hill's so Earl had not been there before. However, the Golden Rule that every sales person should know his territory was very important to Dave Michels. Although Earl had gotten written directions from the Zone Manager, he was hesitant to have Dave see him reading them because he did not want to hear the speech about knowing the territory.

Hill's offices were about seventy miles east on the Long Island Parkway, so there was plenty of time for Earl to find time to read his notes. However, as they neared the exit, Earl began to worry about how he could read the directions without being noticed. As they left the Long Island Expressway, Earl spotted a Hill's tractor trailer ahead. This was the perfect solution. Earl would follow the truck to the warehouse, which he knew was next to the offices he was looking for. Every turn that the truck made, Earl was right behind. All of a sudden, the truck made a fast turn into a side road and came to a stop. Earl was right behind. As Earl and Dave looked out of the window, they discovered that the truck had stopped at the entrance to the town's waste disposal center. Earl had no choice but to admit his problem and get directions from the truck driver before making the call. Dave never let Earl forget that trip.

Back in the early sixties, we had an account manager in New York City named Marvin Cohen. Marvin was a terrific salesman, well loved by his co-workers and his wholesale customers. Once, at a huge fund-raising dinner in New York, Marvin was in attendance, listening as the roll progressed asking each of the people present how much he would pledge. When named, each had to stand and state his pledge publicly; this process helped ensure a successful fund-raising campaign. These goal dinners always had plenty of wine and other beverages to loosen up the donors.

We had a wholesale customer named Oscar Shanker. When Oscar's name was called three times in succession with no response, Marvin felt compelled to answer for him. He jumped up, yelled, "Oscar Shanker pledges $1,000," and then sat down. Everybody cheered and clapped. The only problem, of course, was that Oscar Shanker was not there and was not aware of what Marvin had done. Marvin woke the next morning with a terrible concern, "My God! What have I done? Oscar is my best customer, and I've given his money away without even asking him."

Marvin went to see Oscar at his office to explain the events. Oscar forgave him for his impulsive gesture, and Marvin continued to represent McCormick & Company very effectively for a long time in the New York market.

At another New York fund-raising meeting, we had been assured that there would be no solicitation at the dinner. Immediately after dinner, the roll call began. When it got around to the M's and "What does McCormick & Company pledge," one of our smart young guys jumped up and said, "McCormick pledges the same as last year!" There were cheers, and the roll call continued. One of our sales managers leaned over to ask the McCormick pledger what we had given the year before. The answer was, "Nothing!"

Dorsey Baldwin tells one on General Manager Dave Michels:

> **Having just been promoted to Vice President of Sales for the McCormick/Schilling Division in 1980, I accompanied Dave Michels to Los Angeles to meet the trade.**
>
> **After days of breakfasting, lunching, dining, and meeting with Bill Christy of Certified, Pat Collins of Ralph's, Bill DiVilla of Von's, Roger Hughes of Hughes Markets, and other illustrious grocerymen of Southern California, we planned a quiet evening of only McCormick/Schilling people. In attendance were John Donnelly, Regional Sales Manager; Joe Wertzberger, Zone Manager; Jack Loomis, V.P. Trade Relations; and Dave and myself.**

Joe selected a restaurant called Pomona Valley Mining Company, which sits high on the hills overlooking San Gabriel Valley. After a wonderful dinner, complemented by several bottles of California wine, the waiter presented our check. A few minutes later, the waiter returned for his payment. Seeing the American Express card, he stammered, "Sorry, but we don't accept that card here." Dave, winking at us, took charge. "Well, this is the *only* payment that we can make!" The waiter, gasping, said, "We'll take cash or a personal check." Voices were getting louder and more perplexed. The waiter sashayed away.

Dave was full of himself as he talked about the retreating high-pitched waiter. Fifteen minutes later, the waiter returned and asked if Dave could come into the next room, where the bartender would handle his request and accept his American Express card. Dave triumphantly walked from the table, knowing he had won.

As he entered the lobby, there stood two of "California's finest," and he was threatened with arrest unless he complied with cash. Sheepishly returning to our table, Dave asked how much cash we had.

Later, reclining in the back seat of our car with hands in my now empty pockets, I was amused by the sign that said, "Welcome to Los Angeles."

More from Dorsey:

Back in the year 1976, my wife Maureen and I attended the United International Distributors Convention at the Fairmont Hotel in New Orleans. This annual event was second only to the National Restaurant Show in Chicago in importance of trade/customer participation at a food-service event.

John Shephard had just recently resigned from McCormick and had gone to work for our competitor, Doxsee. Roger Houle attended with me since he had recently been promoted to John's former position as National Accounts Manager. Curt Patterson also was in attendance since the site of the convention, New Orleans, was in his region, the Southeast.

After the annual banquet, our dinner guests, Pat and

Conrad Reuschneck of Behrorst, the largest distributor in Pittsburgh, mentioned how much they craved to go to see The Fifth Dimension, who were performing at the Fairmont that evening. Curt Patterson immediately left to see about tickets. Meeting us in the lobby, Curt told us that it was a sellout. Disappointment covered Pat's face. Undaunted, Roger was dispatched, knowing that we must have tickets at all costs and it must be done with great haste because the 9:30 show was about to begin.

As we arrived at the maitre d's desk, we were greeted by the smiling, but red, and perspiring, round Frenchman's face of Roger Houle. "Hurry, the show is beginning! They are setting up our table now! You won't believe what it cost me," Roger stammered.

We slowly strode into the very well appointed compact club as the announcer called out The Fifth Dimension to the well-known sound of "Up, Up and Away." Suddenly, we were at the stage. At the end of the applause, the lead singer, Billy Davis, nonplussed at seeing the table being placed on the stage in front of the front row table, uttered, "This must be some heavy duty group!"

As we sat down ready to enjoy the show, I glanced around, only to see the scowling face of competitor John Shephard.

But Dorsey did not tell us the one about his introduction to Boston. He had just joined the Food Service Division and was sent up to New England to spend a week with Roger Houle. When he arrived, Roger said, "Dorsey, I hear you're really something and that you like to have a little nightlife. We'll have some fun while you're up here." After working all day, Roger proceeded to take Dorsey out on the town that night – all night. He delivered Dorsey at the hotel in time to shower and meet one of the salesmen for the day. Roger picked Dorsey up again after work and they proceeded to spend the night out again. Next day, another salesman for Dorsey – next night, Roger again.

When Dorsey could no longer stand up straight, he told Roger he had an emergency and needed to get home a day early. Roger, being the gentleman that he is, agreed to Dorsey's leaving early.

But he never told Dorsey until long afterward that after dropping Dorsey off at the hotel every morning all week, Roger went home for a nice long nap!

Years later Dorsey was made National Sales Manager for the Food Service Division. His first act was to call Roger Houle. After preliminaries, Roger asked Dorsey why he was calling. Reply: "Just wanted to tell you I'm your new boss!"

The sales scene now moves Southwest with Bo Kitchens, who began his career with McCormick in New Mexico:

> I began my career with McCormick & Company in New Mexico. During my second week on the job my schedule took me to Gallup, to call on Kimbell Wholesale. Of course, Gallup is in Navajo Indian territory.
>
> The buyer at Kimbell was one of the toughest men I had ever called on before or since. All salespersons referred to him as "Mr. Mack."
>
> After making the call and returning to my car, I found that I had not locked the car doors. Consequently, a drunken Indian man was lying on the front seat with his legs hanging from the passenger side. Unable to wake him or remove him from the car, I returned to the Kimbell office to summon the police.
>
> Noticing my return, Mr. Mack inquired as to the problem. After my explanation, he immediately left his desk and proceeded to the door, instructing me to follow. On the way to my car he picked up a large flat rock that must have weighed at least three pounds. To my surprise, he hit the Indian man on the shin of his right leg, making a horrible cracking sound. The man came up from the car seat holding his leg and hopped away across the parking lot. Mr. Mack turned to me and cautioned me about locking my */?!# car doors in the future.

Schilling General Manager Jack Sassard knew how to turn on an audience. At a key sales meeting, he brought the house down, but not the way he intended. He was standing with arms folded at the back of the room, waiting to be called on for his part of the show. He had an exploding pen in his pocket that he was going to use to get the meeting started with a bang. The pen exploded, all right – in his pocket. It not only blew out the pocket, but it set his suit on fire! The noise, smoke, and confusion broke up the meeting before it started. Jack had done it again. Nobody ever forgot that meeting.

Funny things also happened to salesmen calling on us. After John Scelsa retired from Cal-Compack Foods, he signed on with Gilroy Foods. This story, however, reflects a Scelsa sales call on McCormick spice buyer Tom Burns at the Light Street building in the early 1970s:

> Broaching a delicate subject, Scelsa opens the conversation.
>
> SCELSA: How can I ever interest you in trying our quality American paprika; just a teensy-weensy order?
>
> BURNS: Well, as you know, we have been buying Spanish paprika for a hundred years.
>
> SCELSA: Would it be at all possible for you to convert at least a portion of your needs to American paprika?
>
> BURNS: Well, our packages have the words "Imported Paprika" on all of them.
>
> SCELSA: Wouldn't now be a time to switch at least a portion of your needs to American paprika, a California product, and eliminate the word "Imported" when you order new containers?

Burns is thinking to himself, "This guy is too much. Where did he come from?" But he answered the questions.

> BURNS: Not an easy concept to sell to McCormick, which is so high on Top Quality Products! We give the customer the best!
>
> SCELSA: Can I give you some arguments in favor of American paprika?

(It might be noted here that Scelsa had been known to carry a small silk red, white, and blue American flag which he would occasionally wave as he described the origin of his paprika.)

BURNS: Try giving me at least three good arguments in favor of your domestic stuff.

SCELSA: Please, Tom, it's American paprika! Okay, I've actually got four or five. To begin with, you have to buy all your Spanish once a year, so then you need to store it for long months. You have storage charges, interest costs, color losses, and, most important you run the risk of serious insect and rodent infestation. A terrible thing, Tom! You have none of those problems with American paprika, and further –.

At this point, Tom's phone rings. I offer to step out while Tom talks on the phone. "Absolutely not," he says courteously. "Stay where you are!"

One cannot avoid comprehending the gist of this one-sided phone conversation, which goes like this:

"Is that right? Infestation? Paprika? How bad? I mean how many pounds? From 80 to 120,000? Is it at all salvageable? How can that be? A total loss!! Okay, Jim. We'll talk later."

Tom puts the phone back in its cradle. Long silence, then:

BURNS: Okay, Scelsa, about that American paprika.

SCELSA: Come on, Tom. It's almost five. Let's go somewhere for a few!

There are a lot of ways to sell. When I was Sales Promotion Manager, I bought most of our point-of-sale material from two fierce competitors. One of these hustlers was a fellow by the name of Al May. A New Yorker, he was tough and savvy. He came in one day and to needle him, I took him into the merchandising laboratory, where a just-delivered color proof of his competitor's fall vanilla display point-of-sale card was lying in the middle of the floor. We had tried something new, using elegant black-and-white photography with only the vanilla package itself being in color. It worked and was beautiful. I was very proud of it and described the thinking behind the treatment to Al May. He said, "Piece of – – – !" and with that walked on the proof, shuffled his feet back and forth on it, and then walked over to my office to await my amazed arrival.

Chuck Graham has a long McCormick history, having been a most successful sales executive. He also definitely qualified as one of our "characters." Read his lips:

Shortly after my tenure as Junior Salesman in Washington, D.C., I was transferred as Senior Salesman to Bluefield, West Virginia. Obviously, coming out of Washington, D.C. into Bluefield, West Virginia was like coming out of day into night. However, this was my first big chance as Senior Salesman.

One of the very first calls I made was on Junior Smith's Supermarket in Tazewell. After I introduced myself to Mr. Smith, he requested that I write an order for his next shipment. Well, I wrote the order and noticed that he had about twenty-five dozen 4-ounce vanilla on the top shelf. All I could think of was, "Boy, the guy before me sure loaded this dude down with a lot of 4-ounce vanilla, so I won't put any on this order for sure."

When I turned the order over to Mr. Smith he said, "Did you order me any 4-ounce vanilla?" And I said, "No sir, you have plenty on the shelf." He said, "Order me about twenty cases – these coal miners drink it instead of booze, and I don't want to run out of stock." During my stay in West Virginia, he was one of my best vanilla customers.

I spent a lot of time working the coal fields out of Bluefield, West Virginia, and I called on U.S. Steel's company stores that were located right at the mine sites. For those who do not know what a coal mine company store is, they handle everything from automobiles to coffins. You don't use U.S. currency to buy anything at the company store; you use company scrip, which is printed and issued to you on payday. So obviously everything you buy, you buy at the company store.

I was in U.S. Steel's Grundy, Virginia company store one morning, in the process of writing an order. The manager of the company store explained that he had about fourteen bottles of lemon extract that were only about half full;

the rest had evaporated. He asked me to make sure that I ordered lemon extract on his next order coming from Baltimore. Since there was no other way to supply this particular store, I told the manager that I would fill several of the bottles full from the half-empty ones. Hopefully, this would hold him until the new shipment came in.

Well, everything was going along fine until this man came up to the counter, watched me pouring one bottle into another, and asked, "What do you think you are doing?" My answer was (in a very curt manner), "Well, it looks like I'm pouring one bottle into the other, doesn't it?" Obviously this did not sit well with the stranger, because his next statement was, "Yankee, can you read?" And I said, "I sure hope so." At that point in time, he pulled a badge out of his coat pocket and laid it on the counter. I picked it up and the official badge said State of West Virginia Health Department. The next comment from the stranger was, "How would you like to go to jail for violating the State Pure Foods Act?"

Obviously this old Yankee became very friendly and told the Officer of the State that I felt a credit for the lemon extract was in order and would be issued immediately to the store. He left the store, and to this date, I have never again poured one bottle into another to make a full one.

I had the privilege of introducing our Tio Sancho Mexican foods all over the United States several years back. Although we had all kinds of experiences, one sticks out in my mind the most.

As we all know, McCormick spent a lot of money and time trying to pick the name of our new Mexican food line, and obviously we came up with Tio Sancho. We were introducing our new program down in the Rio Grande Valley, and I called on a gentleman by the name of Mr. Hernandez, who owned about twenty independent stores. After I had finished my presentation, he said, "Señor, do you know what Tio Sancho means?" And I said, "Si, Tio is uncle and Sancho is savior." He said, "It may mean Uncle Savior to you, Señor, but not in the Rio Grande Valley." So I said, "What does it mean, because it cost my company a lot of money to come up with this name." He said, "Tio Sancho is the man who comes in the back door to see your wife when you go out the front door to go to work." I said, "Señor Hernandez, are you kidding me?" He said, "No, I am not kidding you." And I said, "Do you think this will harm our sales?" He said, "Señor, I think it will help it." And it did!

One other experience I had that I would like to share was about the night I spent at the Hyatt Hotel in Germantown, Tennessee (right outside of Memphis). It had been a long day and I didn't get to the hotel until about seven o'clock that evening. I didn't feel much like going down to the dining room for dinner, so I had food sent up. In the past, when I had dinner sent up, I waited until the waiter left my dinner. Then I would take off all my clothes except my shorts and sit back, enjoy my dinner, watch a little television, and really relax.

Well, following the same pattern, I received my dinner, thanked the waiter, undressed down to my shorts, and had a very enjoyable dinner.

If you call room service to pick up your tray, you have to get dressed again, so what I usually did was look out the door both ways up and down the hall. If no one was around, I would quickly step out into the hall, put my tray down, and come back into the room, with no one the wiser.

However, in this particular instance, after I finished eating, I didn't realize that the door had a very strong spring on it, so as I stepped out into the hall in my shorts, the door closed behind me. All I could say was, "Oh, #!!@!!"

I heard people talking in the room next to mine, so I went up and knocked on the door, hoping that they would answer and phone downstairs to have a maid open my door. Obviously they looked through the peep-hole, and all they could see was a man standing there with no clothes on. They probably thought, "He's either wild or he's drunk; don't open the door." In the meantime, several couples passed me in the hall and gave me very strange looks; obviously, all I could do was smile.

My next thought was to get on the elevator, because

there's always a phone in there. Then I thought better of it, because I knew with my luck someone in the lobby would call for the elevator, I would end up in my shorts standing in the lobby, and the only thing I could say would be, "You're not going to believe this!"

Almost in panic, I raced around the hall and came upon a little room that housed the ice and soda machine. Fortunately, there was a house phone in the area. I called the desk, asked them to please send someone up to open my door, and informed them of my situation. I then went back and stood in front of my room – again passing several couples, which was extremely embarrassing. Finally two maids and a security officer came up and opened my door so I could re-enter my room, wearing not much but a red face.

One of the real old-timers who was around way before the Chuck Graham days was Jim McGee, a large, jolly fellow who was Regional Sales Manager in Memphis, Tennessee. The first time I met Jim was on McCormick's Parson Island at a sales meeting, while I was working at the island in a summer job. Jim invited me to come visit him in Memphis, and I said that sounded great. He then asked me what I liked to eat, and when I answered, "Hot Dogs," he got quite excited. He exclaimed, "Hot dogs! Let me tell you something. When you travel with the sales force, you may eat hot dogs, but don't you put hot dogs on your expense account or you'll ruin it for the rest of us. You ate steak."

Long before air conditioning was available in most automobiles, Jim developed a sales technique that worked like magic. On his trips to rural areas, Jim leased a limo with air conditioning and driver. The modus operandi was that the limo would pull up to a small store and the driver would go into the store, leaving Jim in the back seat. The driver would then tell the store owner that Mr. Jim McGee from Memphis was out in the air conditioned limo and had issued an invitation to join him in the car. In the sheltered coolness from the Tennessee heat, Jim and the customer then visited in the limo, while Jim wrote up huge orders for spices, tea, Bee Brand insecticides, and Reliable Brand drugs.

Jim McGee was Regional Sales Manager, Memphis, Tennessee. He eventually joined the Bulk and Institutional Division, which he immediately labeled "Sack Pepper Division."

Joe Waters, who was Clark Barrett's predecessor in trade relations, was traveling with Jim McGee when McGee set up a meeting with the owner/buyer of the area's principal wholesale grocer, commenting to the customer that Joe was a Company director. The customer was about to be presented with our super-truckload deal on McCormick's "free iced tea glass" with 100 tea bags or half a pound of tea.

McGee had alerted Joe Waters to the principal's rare conduct during such an interview. It was okay if he leaned backward in his swivel chair – but if his head touched the wall behind his roll-top desk, "that was the end of the conversation." Joe proceeded to give the sale his level best, but Joe is one of those folks who take a little while just to say "hello." Just as he was getting into high gear, McGee noticed the customer's head closing in on the wall – and without notice pulled the old Doherty trick of feigning a heart attack. The startled customer jumped forward, knocking his cigar into the wastebasket. Joe quickly moved to assist McGee while their friend ran to the water cooler for the standard glass of cool water. Meanwhile, the wastepaper basket caught on fire – in a fitting conclusion to a full-out sales pitch! The end result was an order of 1000 cases of tea and a good-bye handshake.

At about this same period of time, McCormick sales executives attended a meeting in Atlanta. In the evening, up in a hotel room they were playing a little poker, when one of the players decided to stretch his body a little. Standing on his chair, he reached up and grabbed the big ceiling fan, lifting his feet off the chair. One of the guys thought it would be funny to *start* the fan, which he did. Our hero on the fan started to panic, yelling, "Turn off the damn fan." So the switch was turned again, this time into high gear. As our hero's body lifted and got closer and closer to a horizontal position, there was much yelling and screaming and fighting for the control button. A few more seconds without the switch turned off and the crowd down on Peachtree Street would have wondered if it was Superman, hurtling out of the hotel window and flying to the street below.

Yes sir, there were some great peddlers back in the old days, but they have nothing on the modern-day hustlers. One of the great ones is Dave Edington, who has been responsible for bringing many new accounts into the fold. However, nobody wins them all.

Quite a few years ago in the former McCormick Division, we got word that we had lost our business at Delchamps in Alabama.

Dave Edington had the best, though not very close, relationship with Ollie Delchamps, so he placed a call.

Ollie's secretary heard that it was Dave Edington calling and put him right through to Ollie. The initial conversation was much warmer and more personal than expected, as Ollie asked about Dave's family. When Dave turned to the subject of spices, the tone changed immediately. Ollie sounded confused, as he thought he was talking to his *pastor* Dave Edington. When he realized that it was only Dave Edington the spice peddler, Dave got the rather cool response that he (Ollie) would not really be able to help him.

Not all the great McCormick peddlers sell the little 1-ounce size. Al Jones, Vice President - Food Service Sales, has been around the course too:

> When starting my career at McCormick, I was given the responsibility of calling on end-users in the Washington, D.C. market. My job was to demonstrate the quality and the application of McCormick products to chefs in our nation's capital. I must tell you that my first job assignment was most intimidating, since my only culinary experience prior to coming to McCormick was making an angelfood cake when I was in the fifth grade.
>
> Nevertheless, I persevered to the point that John Oxley, my Regional Manager, told me he was adding a distributor to my account responsibility. The account that John wanted me to visit was Mazo Lerch in Alexandria, Virginia. John told me that he did not have their business, that McCormick had some trouble in the past with this account, and that there might be bad feelings.
>
> I immediately made an appointment to see the President, Howard Lerch, the very next week. When I arrived at the account, Mr. Lerch greeted me and took me back to his office. His office was beautifully appointed with a large cherry desk, Oriental rugs, and a mammoth open hearth fireplace on the side wall. Mr. Lerch sat behind his desk and listened to my pitch. Suddenly, he stopped me and asked if I got *The Washington Post*. I said, "No, I live in Columbia, Maryland and get *The Baltimore Sun*."
>
> He said, "Well, let me suggest that you should subscribe to *The Washington Post*, and every day when you come home from work look in the obituary column." He said, "The day you see my name listed in the obituaries, come back and maybe this company would buy from McCormick at that time." Then he got up, shook my hand, and said, "Goodbye."
>
> Several years later, I came back to the Washington market, this time as a regional manager. Once again, we had a "greenhorn" working for us as a territory sales representative, and he expressed his concern calling on Mazo Lerch. Unlike my predecessor, I chose not to send him into the

account alone. Once again, I set up an appointment with Mr. Lerch. As before, he greeted us, and took us to his office. I began my pitch, but this time, I really felt I had my act together. As I spoke, Mr. Lerch listened intently. I really felt my presentation was penetrating his crust and pressed on to make the sale.

About three-quarters of the way through my sales story, Mr. Lerch stood up, picked up his *Wall Street Journal*, and walked from behind the desk toward the door. He continued out the door, until the only sound left in the room was the crackle of the fireplace and the sound of air rushing through the gaping holes of our mouths as we sat wondering what had happened.

The salesman and I waited several minutes until it appeared that Mr. Lerch wasn't coming back. I got up, went outside the office, and asked his secretary if Mr. Lerch was okay. I told her that while in the middle of my presentation he had gotten up and walked out. The secretary looked at her watch and said, "No, I'm sure that Mr. Lerch is fine; he just went to lunch." The salesman and I left Mazo Lerch and later sat in the car reassessing our objectives for this account.

One of the great treats of being Vice President of Sales is having the opportunity to travel to Hawaii. Although we do a considerable amount of business on the islands, I've only had two occasions to go there. I remember being told once that Bob Hassel, a former National Sales Manager, visited Hawaii and got into trouble while lying on the beach during the afternoon of a work day. Unfortunately, as the story goes, McCormick Chairman Harry Wells and wife Lois, while vacationing on the same island, came across Bob as they strolled down the beach.

Keeping Bob's fate in the back of my mind, I traveled to Honolulu for a food show several years ago. While in Hawaii I contacted Leslie Murakami, our Territory Sales Representative, to set up a meeting for me to visit Mr. Hata, President of Y. Hata, our largest distributor in the islands. Leslie hesitated and expressed his concern that Mr. Hata was very odd and most likely would not wish to see anyone from Baltimore. I insisted that I see him, if only to wish him well and thank him for his business. Leslie finally acquiesced and set up the meeting.

On the way to see Mr. Hata, Leslie filled me in on how badly Mr. Hata treated outsiders. As if Leslie's description of Hata wasn't bad enough, he told me that there was one other thing I had to remember. He said that Mr. Hata had a very mean dog that stayed behind his desk and no matter what happened, I should not look at the dog. As we got out of Leslie's car, I told him not to worry, that dog or no dog, I had been in tough situations before and I was sure that this call would be a piece of cake.

As we entered Mr. Hata's office, I was surprised to see several office clerks working in the same room where the great Hata sat. We approached the back of the room where, behind a desk filled with stacks of paper, we found Mr. Hata quietly reviewing invoices. A table next to Mr. Hata's desk was filled with samples left by salesmen who I envisioned had long forgotten their hopes of ever making a sale. We quietly stood in front of Hata's desk like two schoolboys waiting to be acknowledged by the headmaster. Hata would not look up unless we spoke. However, somewhere close to my left side, I clearly heard the growl of a dog. I remembered Leslie telling me not to look at the dog, but the dog was close and I thought that I should at least scan the room to get a quick fix on where he was.

Maybe it was fate or maybe my eyes had a mind of their own. Nevertheless, as my eyes looked to my left, they connected with the eyes of the ugliest, meanest dog on the Hawaiian Islands. As my eyes remained fixed on the dog's eyes, he began to show his teeth, and move toward my left leg. Fortunately, a clerk sitting close to the dog yelled out, "No! No!" With that she reached in her desk drawer and pulled out a bright yellow tennis ball. As the dog lunged towards me, the clerk threw the ball into the air, and the dog, without taking his eyes off me, opted to bite the ball instead of my leg. The dog then dropped the ball and continued to come once again toward me until the clerk tossed the ball to divert his attention. Once again, the dog decided to bite the ball instead of me.

Meanwhile, Mr. Hata had not spoken nor, in fact, showed any emotion at all as he continued to correct invoices. Finally, after several more minutes, which seemed like hours to me, Mr. Hata grunted. At first I thought Hata had burped, but Leslie seemed to take the cue and with that, he introduced me. At this point, I thought brevity would be best, not only because of the dog, but because Hata had still not looked up from his invoices. I quickly said, "Mr. Hata, I just wanted to tell you that I have been wanting to meet you and that I am particularly glad that I didn't meet your dog first." Mr. Hata grunted, which I took as acceptance of my humor, but certainly there was no interest in developing a long-term relationship. I then said, "I'm sure that Leslie will be able to take care of all your needs for McCormick, and I want you to know that we appreciate your business." Mr. Hata grunted again and with that, I turned and walked out.

Leslie remained for another twenty minutes in Hata's office as I pulled myself together in the parking lot. Finally, Leslie came out with a look that was troubled. Leslie informed me that after I had left the room, Hata complained that another distributor on the island had a flyer promoting McCormick products at a discount. He said that the flyer made Hata mad and he was throwing McCormick out. I couldn't believe it and immediately wanted to go back and try to save the account.

I told Leslie that I was even willing to let Hata's dog chew up my leg if that would help. Leslie said no and that I would just have to understand their culture; when it is over, it is over. Leslie drove me back to the airport for my return flight to Baltimore. As we reached the parking lot, Leslie said, "I'm sorry. I have lost our biggest account. I will resign." I said, "Please, Leslie. Don't commit hara-kiri, and don't worry." I was sure we would get Hata's business back.

As I boarded the plane, I reflected on the events that had just transpired. I couldn't, for the life of me, figure why anyone would ever want to go to Hawaii. Two weeks after my visit, and without any fanfare, we received our next order from Hata, and we have kept his business ever

since. I have only been back to Hawaii one other time.
That time, I told Leslie I'd just send my best to Mr. Hata
and his dog.

Al Jones also worked once with former Southeast Regional
Manager Curt Patterson, calling on the director of purchasing for
the Nashville City schools.

Curt made an excellent pitch on the quality of McCormick
spices. Northerner Jones listened intently to Curt's Southern
drawl as he pressed the buyer to specify McCormick. Suddenly,
the buyer leaned forward and said that his wife had recently purchased some McCormick paprika at home and that they had discovered bugs in the product. Without missing a beat, Curt replied
that quite often during the summer time, little "orgasms" would
be found in paprika. Jones first thought that the Southern drawl
had confused him and that Curt was really referring to organisms.
But Curt went on to say that in addition to paprika, one might
find orgasms in jars of red pepper or cayenne.

The smiling buyer responded with, "Then I guess I'll have to
tell my wife to go out and buy some more of those spices."

Some days you can't lose!

Peddlers love to bet, possibly because they are so competitive.
Our products group back in the '60s was made up of ex-peddlers.
Two of them were promoted to other positions, and we decided
that an evening on the town to celebrate was in order. The two
graduates, Carl Holmes and Bill Hetherington, challenged each
other to a martini-drinking contest – and a raucous evening was
guaranteed. After surviving a loud dinner at Oriole pitcher Milt
Pappas's restaurant, we moved a few blocks to the hottest spot in
town, the Downtowner Club.

A lady entertainer was playing the piano on a little stage, and
the place was in full swing. The martini contest continued. Bill
Hetherington really got into the mood and stood up on our table
to do a little dance. He fell off, but Tom Miller and R.J. Crampton
helped him back up. The crowd roared, and the lady entertainer
broke into a big grin and encouraged Bill. She then changed the
tune to "The Stripper" and Bill really got into the routine. He
took off his coat, then his tie, then his shirt. The crowd went wild.

As the song was concluding, Bill was smiling as much as the entertainer – but then as Bill took off his belt in mock striptease – his pants fell to the table.

Still undulating in his jockey shorts, Bill was unfazed. But the entertainer's expression changed from smile to horror and anger. She yelled, "Out! Out!" and yelled for the management to call the cops. We got out just ahead of the police, but not before declaring Holmes the winner of the martini contest. Hetherington had obviously disqualified himself.

The decision was to be reversed, however. About 3:30 the next morning, a distraught Holmes called my home. He was still downtown, having forgotten where he had parked his car. I wasn't much help. I told him that he had not only lost his car, but the martini contest as well, and hung up!

Larry Hockman from the Industrial sales side was also out late one night. In fact, the sun was coming up when he arrived home. Thinking quickly, Larry undressed down to his shorts, threw his clothes into the car, and marched up to his front door. Picking up the morning newspaper, he rang the bell and pounded on the door until his wife answered. She was very sympathetic when he told her that the door slammed shut just as he was picking up the morning paper!

Old soldiers may never die and just fade away, but old salesmen may die but never fade away.

Milt van den Berg attended the funeral services of a recently deceased member of the sales force. He was not one of the most popular colleagues. As Milt sat down, he asked the person next to him, "I wonder how long the service will be?" His neighbor answered, "I really don't know, but they've planned a fifteen-minute eulogy and an hour-and-a-half rebuttal!"

Chapter Six

Parson Island

During World War II, the Company purchased a 200-acre island called Parson Island on the Crab Alley section of the Eastern Shore of Maryland for the purpose of experimentally farming herbs and spices and for the testing of new formulas of insecticides. At the end of the war, the island was used for various meetings in the renovated farm house and for entertaining customers during hunting or fishing season. Employees, at their own expense, could reserve vacation time. A big annual event was the Sales Board meeting, a week-long affair highlighted by a day of competition; entertainment, which consisted of the initiation of new Sales Board members into the Royal Order of Seagoing Honkers; and a crab feast for all the McCormick management boards.

During the first summer seasons of our ownership of Parson Island, teenage boys were hired as summer help. I was fortunate to be one of them. The tenant farmer was a super guy by the name of Joe Usilton. He was an old Eastern Shorer who had grown up on the island. Joe was smart, nature-savvy, and a hard worker. He was also a good hunter and fisherman, with the kind of personality that all the guests enjoyed. Joe had the brains in his family and employed his brother, Jack, as a hand who did most of the heavy work. While Joe was a small man, Jack was very large and wore only overalls and bare feet. No laundry bill for him!

We were setting up the bedrooms in the main house attic one afternoon before the Sales Board arrived the next day. I happened to look out the front window as Jack was towing the Island Barge

Parson Island created many great memories for McCormick employees, customers and friends. Vice Chairman Grayson Luttrell was elected "mayor" of the island.

across the inlet towards a pier in front of the house. The water was quite shallow in most spots, and I could see that Jack was not in the channel. The barge was carrying a wagon load of coal. Suddenly, the barge stopped, the tow line snapped, the wagon pitched forward, and the whole load of coal went into the Chesapeake Bay.

One summer we had a cook, Tom, who prepared meals for the summer help, and what a character he was! A talkative man from New Jersey who didn't cook too well but had an incredible ego. He bragged to us that he could do this or that and claimed he was a great oarsman with the rowboat, and also a great ladies' man.

One Saturday night, he went into town for a night with the ladies at the local saloon. We took him ashore and left him a rowboat for his return. The distance across the water was only about a quarter of a mile. However, unbeknownst to old Tom, we had

Joe Usilton, an Eastern Shore native, presided over Parson Island as a guide, and congenial duck hunting and fishing companion to all guests.

tied a bucket on the bottom of the boat. Suspended by a rope tied to both sides of the rowboat, this made a perfect sea anchor no matter which way the boat was rowed. What should have been a fifteen-minute row took him two and a half hours in the middle of the night; and the best part of it was the next day, when he described his tough voyage in detailed amazement with no idea what had caused his problem.

The same rowboat was used because the tide was too low for the motorboat to get to the mainland dock when some Factory Board members arrived for a Parson Island Sales Board meeting. As Plant Superintendent Gus Walters, who had Coke-bottle lenses in his rimless glasses, jumped down into the rowboat, his legs sprang in reaction, and he plunged overboard into two feet of water. A good start on the day.

Sales board member Irv Horowitz wanted to catch some crabs, which were in light supply that year. He had never crabbed, so several of the boys gathered a crowd and told Irv to get in the water with a net while the crowd looked for crabs from the pier. He caught a dead crab, which was put into a large pail. Then the crab was thrown into the water on the other side of the pier. To a chorus of "Irv! over here" shouts, Irv scrambled in the

Another group boards the boat bound for Parson Island.

three-foot-deep water, went under the pier to the other side, and gingerly scooped up the dead crab. With a prideful grin, he put the crab in the bucket. The process was then repeated on the other side of the pier. Irv must have caught that same dead crab twenty times; but as they carried the bucket up to the clubhouse ahead of him, he never caught on until he was proudly trying to show his catch to the entire assemblage and discovered that his real catch consisted of only one dead crab!

Another year, Irv wanted to shoot some skeet, so he was taken down on the front lawn in front of the pier. He raised his gun and the target was released, but Irv was late in tracking it. As the target came back down, Irv wheeled around ninety degrees and fired point-blank into the oncoming tractor being driven by big Jack Usilton. How he missed Jack I'll never understand, but Jack seemed as oblivious to the whole episode as Irv was.

The highlight of the Sales Board outing was always the Honkers initiation. Named after "honking" geese, this organization was initiated by C.P. as an excuse to have some entertainment

New "Honkers" were initiated in a series of traditional rituals.

at these outings. When fresh initiates ran out, a new, higher-level organization called the Seagoing Honkers was formed so that everyone could be initiated again. Ultimately, the Royal Order of Seagoing Honkers was the most elite organization.

Special Company paraphernalia, carefully prepared by Buck Burton's shop, was dragged out once a year for the occasion. The initiates were dressed up in white coveralls and were blindfolded during portions of the show. One prop was a phone booth, into which an initiate was sent to answer the ringing phone. When the receiver was picked up, the unsuspecting victim was sprayed with water full blast through the speaker via the garden hose, which was hooked up to it. A two-story wire bin was opened to hold several initiates on the bottom half and several on the top. The top was filled with eggs. The upper crew was directed to crawl around and smash the eggs which, of course, ran down on the group below. After this rather messy operation, the whole crew was washed down via garden hose and told to relax and sit down on the series of specially rigged, attached wooden chairs. Just about when they started to relax amid all the frivolity, an electric shock was sent through the chairs . . . and the initiates! Each group of four chairs was individually wired so the operators could alternate the electric charge. The result looked like a human demonstration of Mexican jumping beans!

Noting that some of the men might be getting hungry by now, we blindfolded them and directed them to eat what they were served. It was spaghetti. However, before the blindfolds came off, the plates were exchanged for ones with cut-up bloodworms. Never was a bad temper displayed, and as juvenile as this might seem today, a rollicking, good time was had by all. Touch football, softball, and volleyball games were also part of the program.

Doug Reed, Vice President Manufacturing, administers a "Honkers" welcome.

These were not so tame, and quite frequently, someone ended up in the hospital. In my own "last" football game, my nose got moved about an inch to the right.

Billy Hillenbrand, an All-American at Indiana and starting halfback for the early Baltimore Colts, had the greatest hip fake in football. Billy became a regional sales manager for McCormick but eventually left because he hated flying. He was caught between bases at one of the outing's softball games and gave his famous fake to the fellow holding the ball, who promptly fell on his face. Billy calmly stepped over him and walked on to second base.

Lloyd Moore, another regional manager, was a semi-pro pitcher who made the outside vs. inside management game a farce one year. Nobody could see the ball when Lloyd pitched, and it wasn't any fun. So the next year, we made a new rule to trap Lloyd. The rule: Anyone leaving his position for an inning couldn't play that position again. C.P. couldn't attend the meeting that year, and we arranged for him to call Lloyd shortly after the game started. C.P. congratulated Lloyd on the great job he was doing, and Lloyd returned to the game – this time in the outfield.

That was the year that six of us from the home office took my sailboat down from Annapolis. We departed Parson Island in the evening after the usual crab feast. As we hoisted sail, Armando Sargenti, Sales Board member from New Jersey, was telling the group on shore, "If that boat goes down, we can afford to hire two hundred new salesmen."

Red Elliott remembers his first Sales Board meeting as an associate member. His sponsor was J.P. Bergenon from New Orleans. He slept in a little white house behind the main house, where there was only one bathroom for the six people in the house. The first morning, everyone was first-second-third-fourth-fifth and Red was number six to use the bathroom. Red got ready and walked to breakfast at the big main house. Everyone was having breakfast when he walked in. Carter Parkinson, who was Vice President of Sales at that point, asked out loud, "Who is Red's sponsor?" J. P. said, "I am." "Then take him aside and advise him we serve breakfast at 8:00 A.M. No one is to be late or they can go home. Do you understand, Red Elliott?" asked Carter. The next four mornings, Red was first to use the bathroom, to get dressed, and report to breakfast.

Actually Red was lucky. At a regional sales meeting one year in the Little Theater at the Light Street building, Carter was starting off the meeting from the stage when one of the retail men walked in late. Carter stopped and said, "Young man, if you can't get to work on time, you don't belong in this company," and fired him on the spot. The guy looked like a startled deer caught between automobile headlights.

But Red survived for another meeting, this one his second visit to Parson Island. Red recalls:

> We left to go back to Light Street on Thursday afternoon. We had a closing Sales Board meeting dinner. After we had all been seated at our table and the food was being served, someone threw a roll that hit my tie and bounced onto the table. I picked up the roll and dipped it in the brown gravy and drew back to throw it at the person who threw it at me (Charlie McCormick). Someone sitting at my table said, "What are you going to do?" I said, "I am going to throw the roll back." This person said, "No, no, we don't do that to Charlie." I said, "I do," threw the roll, and hit Charlie in the middle of his tie (bull's-eye). It got so quiet you could hear a pin drop. Charlie got up. He said, "Red, stand up." It got even quieter. He continued, "You are the only person who ever had the guts to throw back . . . congratulations." He then asked everyone to stand and give me a standing ovation.

There are many stories about Red:
"(Hot damn y'all – I'll declare) Texans must be tough."

> At one time there was a hat throwaway game played. If you were in a cab with other McCormick sales people, having fun was to grab a hat off a friend and throw it out the cab window, or take a hat off a friend and throw it out in the street while walking down the street. One time, we were coming back to the mainland on the boat from Parson

Island and someone threw a hat off a friend's head into the water – then another – then another. One person said, "Put your hand on your hat, Red." I said, "The one who throws my hat into the water will get thrown body and all into the water." Guess what? I did not lose my hat. Thrown away hats were always replaced by a check. We had lots of fun and laughs.

Red wasn't always so lucky. The Sales Board was considering a project concerning red food color. Samples of red food color were all over the meeting room, and Bob Sharman, then Zone Manager in Miami, used one of the pints of color to pull a prank on Red. While Red was showering in the morning prior to the meeting, Sharman snuck into the shower stall next to Red's with a bottle of red food color and poured it on Red as he showered. Red bolted from the shower, of course in the nude, screaming that he was bleeding. Much to his chagrin, a smiling Sharman stepped out of the next shower with the food-color bottle . . . to the delight of the now assembled Sales Board members.

Lloyd Lawson, Houston Zone Manager, was also a victim of Sharman's madness. Lloyd was staying down in one of the adjacent cabins on the island when Sharman found a dead owl. While Lloyd was up in the main house one evening, Sharman went into Lloyd's cabin and propped the owl up on the toilet. Late in the evening, Lloyd came back after a long card game and a "lot of refreshments." When he went into the bathroom, he saw the owl, screamed, ran out of the cabin, and yelled to the island manager, Joe Usilton, who was just closing up the main house for the night. Lloyd yelled, "There's an owl on my toilet." Joe yelled back, "Well, you'll just have to wait till the owl's finished. There's nothing I can do about it!"

But Sharman got his at the end of the trip, when he almost missed the boat to the mainland. As the boat was leaving the pier, Sharman ran and jumped, landing on the bow but sliding across it. He grabbed the anchor to hold onto and went over the side, anchor and all. You can bet nobody laughed – oh, no!

The Sales Board wasn't the only group to frequent the island. In the spring of each year, the Multiple Management Boards from

Baltimore would go to the island for a day of recreation and a night of eating, drinking, and games.

Usually, there were three party types at these outings: those who went to bed early, at about midnight; those who went to bed late, around 2:00 A.M.; and those who would stay up all night. One night, the all-nighters decided that *everyone* should stay up all night and about 3:00 A.M. tried to rouse the rest of the group.

They were only moderately successful and were completely unsuccessful in arousing three or four board members sleeping in one of the cabins. Some revelers climbed up on the roof and were jumping up and down like Santa Claus. Others were busily emptying aerosol cans of room deodorant through screen windows. Others were making sounds of wild animals, but nothing worked.

Finally, one had a bright idea of faking a fire. He sprayed lighter fluid on the screen windows, lit it, and yelled, "Fire!" However, the fluid had gone through the screen onto the curtains. There was a fire! The awakening was a success, but it almost burned down the cabin in the process.

Incidentally, one of Sharman's favorite tricks was to yell, "Fire!" whenever he passed a ladies' room. Sometimes he'd open the door a little as he did it!

Ted Foti of the Flavor Division tells of a group from the Light Street office who went to the island for a couple of days' personal fishing trip. In the warm summer evening, the house got warm, and the group decided to cool off with a drive around the island in the island jeep. It was cooler in the nude, and off they went. However, the battery was dead, so they decided to jumpstart the jeep by pushing it. The jeep had a trailer attached to it. One person, whom Foti won't name (could it be Ted?*), was pushing from behind the jeep and in front of the trailer. As the jeep lurched forward, he fell to the ground and was run over by the trailer. He

---

*Having heard that he, Ted Foti, had been accused of being the hero of his own story, Ted finally decided to tell the truth and reveal the identity of "scar buns." Late on the evening of the 1992 Board party at The Hunt Valley Inn, Ted, in a weakened condition following his successful dietary loss of 106 pounds, blurted out, "It was Bob Murphy!" (currently General Manager of the Food Service Division).

C. P. addresses the "Honkers." There was always time for fun once the business discussions were over.

was taken to the mainland to receive a couple dozen embarrassing stitches in his derriere.

And then there was McCormick Ingredients General Manager Randy Jensen who, when entertaining customers during duck-hunting season, placed his shotgun against the wall. It discharged, shooting a hole in the porch roof of the cabin. Randy, embarrassed, said nothing about the incident on his return to the office, but you can't keep good information from leaking. At the Flavor Division Christmas party, Jim Albrecht, then Vice President and General Manager of the Flavor Division, presented a few routine C.P. McCormick Awards. Then, with great solemnity, he presented the First Annual Roof Duck Award to Jensen. The prestigious award consisted of a rubber chicken nailed to a pine board.

It's hard to remember, but there were days when Company

cars had no air conditioning. This subject was placed on the Sales Board agenda. The fellows from the South were rather emotional about the upcoming discussion, but board members from the extreme North were reluctant to go on record for requesting additional expense that they felt in all probability would have little effect on sales.

The subject was scheduled for after lunch. It was normal procedure for the island group, after eating one of cook Henrietta's fine Eastern Shore meals, to take a little walk around the front lawn of the main house. It was a beautiful view and, if a bit of a breeze was blowing, quite refreshing on a summer day. This day, the thermometer read in the 90s.

When the Board reassembled for the next session, the room was hot and stuffy. Someone had switched off the air conditioning. As a move was made to switch it back on, New Orleans

The favorite game was always gin – and it was serious!
(l-r): Ed Crone, Harvey Reinecker, Louie Towt, Paul Frisch.

Zone Manager J.P. Bergenon shouted in his deep Marine sergeant voice, "Leave that switch off. I'm leading the next subject and it has to do with air conditioning for the Company automobiles. I want all of you from the North to experience just how it feels down South without air conditioning."

That's how all our fleet cars became air conditioned.

Special guests were sometimes invited to the island to hunt. One was Eddie Erdelatz, former All-Pro for the San Francisco '49ers and later head coach at the U.S. Naval Academy. Eddie got out early to hunt wild birds and saw some action near the small pond that was in the middle of the island. In true military manner, he hit the ground and with his shotgun held perpendicular, he crawled about three hundred yards through the underbrush before jumping up and blasting the hell out of a few tame turkeys being raised for Thanksgiving sale.

Another guest arrived one evening when several executives and their wives were playing cards after dinner. There was a knock on the front door, and there stood a Navy aviator in full flying regalia but soaking wet. The engine had failed on his plane, and he had ditched in the Bay right off the island and swum ashore.

Have you ever wondered where the term wild-goose chase came from? Well, Joe Usilton taught me one day when he took me out on a small inboard that belonged to the island. His goal was to catch a goose so that he might clip its wings and put it in the pond with other "tame" geese. This was illegal, but often practiced by hunters to draw other geese to the area.

The only time of year that you have a chance of catching a goose is when they lose many of their feathers just before growing new ones. When in this condition, try as they might, they can't get airborne. What they can do, however, is flap their wings and skim over the water at a high speed. However, they can only go a short distance before tiring.

So Joe took out the boat, found a lone goose, and proceeded to chase him. With today's faster boats, it would be easier. Every time the goose would tire and sit down in the water, Joe would stalk him, but just before arriving at the goose's position, the goose would take off in another direction. This process went on for well over an hour until the goose tired. Then, when the goose couldn't simulate flight anymore, he dove. He was able to stay under water for several minutes at a time, and we would anticipate where he would surface next and try to be there. Finally, we guessed right and picked the goose out of the water; total time was two and a half hours!

The customer entertainment was effective. Hunters loved the island, and many others spent important holidays there. For a number of years, Chuck Barcelona, president of an unsold account in Buffalo, hunted at the island. A decision was finally made by Chuck to switch to McCormick spices, but he said that he would only give the opening order to his favorite cook, the island's Henrietta. So Henrietta was flown to Buffalo and ushered into Chuck's office while the rest of our crew cooled their heels in the waiting room. That opening order was framed and hung on the main house wall.

After many years of nostalgic service to the Company, its people, customers, and a few invited outside groups, Parson Island was sold in 1988 during a series of reorganizations that were put into place to help us better serve our customers during the last years of the twentieth century.

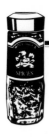

Chapter Seven

A More Formal Organization – John Curlett

When C. P. was asked what his primary responsibility was as President of the Company, he would always answer the same way: "Making sure that my directors work together as a team." With one exception, the senior board (now called the Corporate Board) consisted of the heads of the various departments of the business. Only Board members had "Director" titles. The one outside Board member was Eric Johnston, head of the Motion Picture Association and special ambassador to four U.S. Presidents. In lieu of other outside directors, C.P. chose an advisory council, and these gentlemen were invited to quarterly Board meetings and social functions.

John Curlett was elected President in 1955. The top management team was C.P. McCormick, Chairman; John Curlett, President; Grayson "Pops" Luttrell, Vice Chairman; and Jim Welsh, Secretary. Unfortunately, a man very important to the Company's early success and another "people" person, Treasurer Brooke Furr, passed away in 1955. He was succeeded by Ernie Issel.

The business had progressed and needed a more formal structure than C.P.'s entrepreneurial style. John hired a consultant by the name of Samuel P. Card. Sam was an M.I.T. graduate and a very intelligent and precise guy. He was hired for three months and stayed over three years.

Sam put together the first-ever organizational charts and spent most of his time writing job descriptions, also a first. He also recommended organizational changes. I was Products

John Curlett, "Pops" Luttrell and Dick Hall in a discussion of new products.

Manager at the time, a responsibility similar to today's brand management. Sam and I rode to work together every day, and I was quite interested when he got around to reviewing the products management setup. It only took him a few days of study before on the ride downtown he said, "I'm going to recommend to John Curlett that your operation be disbanded."

Thanks a lot!

He went on to say that he thought I would be a good sales promotion manager and would also recommend that. And that's what happened.

One of the side projects that Sam was asked to do was to come up with a sales incentive plan. He did and when Sam explained it, it was a fantastic plan. It didn't last long, however, because once Sam left the scene, we found it too complex to understand.

Sales promotion was a fun job, and particularly timely for me because we were in the process of introducing a number of new products, and we could now follow them through to the marketplace. "Fun" and "Fluffy" were two of our major product introductions; both were doomed to ultimate failure, but both were successfully launched for a period of time.

"Fluffy" instant mashed potatoes became the number-two brand in the U.S. after R. T. French, which had sold the only instant potato for many years. General Foods actually was the

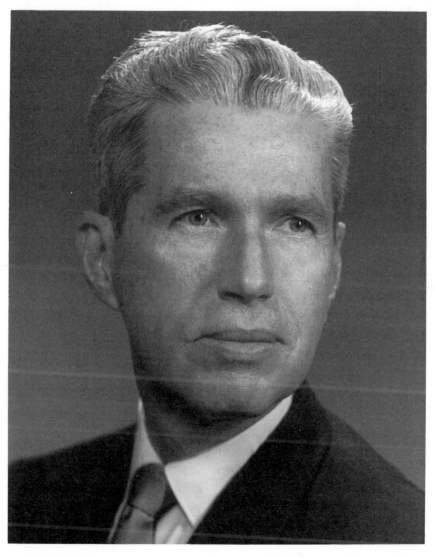

Jim Welsh

Brooke Furr, Treasurer

second company to introduce it, but we had the best product and a good package. We used brokers for the first time in most markets, and distribution was good. The category grew impressively – too impressively. Borden, Pillsbury, and General Mills all came out with competing products. The market wasn't growing fast enough for all of us.

One of our great accounts has always been Publix Markets in Lakeland, Florida. We've always loved that account because of the people culture built by founder George Jenkins. We've always felt that Publix, in many ways, was much like McCormick.

They had been a loyal customer for many years, so I felt good as I walked in their front door with our Fluffy broker one day. We were calling on George Jenkins's brother Charlie, Vice President-Purchasing.

I was loaded for bear, having some beautiful brochures which I had just made up, fresh off the press. They gave market-share information and profitability and certainly "proved that Fluffy was the brand to handle."

But alas, there was trouble in the marketplace. Too many brands and not enough movement. Charlie Jenkins, whom I had not met before, gave me a warm welcome before stating, "If you've come to sell me some Fluffy potatoes, forget it. I wouldn't take any if you gave them to me. I don't need any potatoes."

Nice beginning. Charlie let me go through my presentation; finally, and only at the end, did I see his eyes brighten. Due to the competition, the case allowances had risen considerably, and the current competitive deals had risen to about one free case with

Making big decisions on Fluffy were (l-r): Carter Parkinson, Buzz McCormick, Chuck Mattern, Bud Weiser, Al Ireland, Ed Crone.

five. I told Charlie that he could have one case free with *one*. Having made his initial comment, he was stuck with it, and we said a pleasant goodbye.

The next day, he ordered a lot of Fluffy instant mashed potatoes.

Food manufacturing brass from the North has always invaded Florida in the wintertime. Due to Publix's leadership in the market and their friendliness, Charlie Jenkins was target number one for sales calls. Charlie was down-to-earth, serious, and an expert buyer, but sometimes mischievous. He hated long sales presentations made by pretentious VIPs visiting him.

One such VIP from a major food manufacturer called the local sales representative and insisted that a meeting be set up with Charlie so that he could show him a new line of products. The request was for a *two-hour* meeting. Charlie didn't want to cause the local representative any trouble, so he agreed.

On the appointed date, the presentation was started in Charlie's office, with Charlie, the VIP, and the local representative in attendance. A few minutes into the meeting, the door opened and a gentleman looked in, excused himself, and began to close the door. Charlie called to the fellow, "Sam, please come in, I want you to hear this." Charlie then introduced Sam as the right person to sit in on the presentation. Charlie insisted that Sam sit in his chair to listen to the presentation, while he stepped out for a few minutes to clean up some errands.

Periodically, Charlie would stick his head back in the office, ask how things were going, and insist that Sam listen to the full story. After the presentation, Charlie returned, thanked the VIP for giving Publix Markets the opportunity to hear about his products, and told him they would consider his offer. The VIP was elated, as Sam had seemed very impressed and had nodded approvingly on every important point of the sales pitch. What he didn't know was that Sam was the mail clerk!

After we thought the Fluffy sales pitch at Publix had failed, I went over to Tampa and called on a small, sleepy wholesaler. Real sleepy. And the call was right after lunch. The office was up in an attic over a small warehouse, and again I pitched my heart out for Fluffy potatoes, using the charts and graphs, ads, and all the sales tools that I had at my disposal. When I finished, the buyer finally spoke. He said, "No, I already have a brand of *marshmallows!*"

We employed the Tarrant Brokerage Company in St. Louis. After the initial good distribution was achieved, Fluffy sales spluttered, and we went to St. Louis for a sales meeting. Our Vice President of Sales, Bud Weiser, asked Tom Tarrant to bring in his entire sales force for the meeting. Tom started the meeting and turned it over to Bud. Bud had his usual blue pinstripe power suit on and proceeded to take off his jacket, revealing his wide suspenders over a blue shirt. This meant he was ready to give a major chewing out. And chew he did, just like he would have when he was dissatisfied with his own sales executives.

After a while, Tom interrupted and said, "Bud, would you please step outside with me for a second." They did, indeed, step out and Tom said, "Nobody talks to my sales force that way." They returned and Tom immediately adjourned the meeting, leaving Bud standing in his power suspenders.

Al Ireland and I had made the original Fluffy presentation to Tarrant's group. Al made the presentation, and I made the potatoes. Al made a good presentation, while I proved I couldn't even boil water . . . safely. I boiled the water over!

Some years before, McCormick had opened St. Louis as a spice market. An initial sales crew went in, and then a local sales force was employed. At the end of the initial introductory period, a dinner was held for the new sales force at the ornate and elaborate Chase Hotel. Bud Weiser hosted the dinner and "gentleman" Clark Barrett, Director of Trade Relations, was Master of Ceremonies. After a delicious dinner was served, Clark addressed the group of new, young McCormick sales employees.

Clark was an excellent speaker and always came across as very sincere and interested in everyone's welfare. As he was welcoming the new salesmen and telling them what a great company McCormick was, the maitre d' slipped the bill beside Clark. Clark glanced down and continued his talk. But he glanced back down a second time and abruptly stopped in mid-sentence. He then exclaimed, "#!!a!!, Bud, did you see this bill?" The salesmen laughed. They thought it was a planned routine!

PEPPER PEOPLE

Another important sales meeting took place in Springfield, Massachusetts – actually, two meetings. We acquired the Baker Extract Company of Springfield, Massachusetts in 1962 and set up two sales sessions to announce the new venture. President John Curlett led the delegation and scheduled lunch with the Baker sales force and then a dinner with the McCormick sales force. At the lunch, he met Mike Manaker, the leading Baker sales executive and a thorn in our side for many years. As did the rest of us, John liked Mike immediately and accepted him into the family.

John's speech to both sales groups was focused on the fact that although we had been competitors for many years, these two fine old companies were now one. We needed to forget bygones and work towards the future.

After the McCormick dinner, John was interested in Charlie Doyle's reactions. Charlie was in charge of McCormick's sales in the area. So John asked Charlie, "Have you met Mike Manaker?" Charlie said, "Yes, he's a S.O.B." I'd never seen John so disheartened.

While we were introducing Fluffy, we also were introducing "Fun," the instant soft drink that we knew was going to revolutionize the drink industry. Veteran salesman Al Ireland was in charge of sales for both products, which were being sold by brokers. When he called on the famous head buyer, Bob Pelz, at A&P, Al mixed up a grape flavor "Fun" and served it up in a paper cup, which, unfortunately, leaked not only down the front of the great man's shirt, but also all over his desk. Amazingly, Al got the order, and never got a cleaning bill.

This is the same Al Ireland who, some years before, had made one of his very first calls as a McCormick representative selling mayonnaise. Our mayonnaise formula was a superior one; to demonstrate our quality, the cap was taken off a package and the product turned upside down. It never came out, and ours was the only mayonnaise that could withstand this test.

Well, young Al and Ed Ellis called on the buyer for Read's Drug Stores with the hope of getting McCormick mayonnaise in the entire Read's chain. Ed demonstrated the firmness of our mayonnaise by opening a quart bottle and turning it upside down right in front of the frightened buyer's eyes. It was a warm day. You guessed it. Plop went mayonnaise all over the buyer's desk!

Another account for Kraft!

John Curlett was a very enthusiastic fellow with a great sense of humor. He had been in charge of the flavoring extract department for a number of years and always had a special interest in extracts. He once promoted a pie pan as a premium and ended up with so many pie pans in inventory that he was nicknamed "Pie Pan John" by his associates.

But as President, one day he examined a competitor's bulk vanilla product that was suspected of being adulterated with synthetic vanillin. He remarked, "This product will make the roosters crow, the corn grow, and childbirth a pleasure."

John's years as President were not easy. Like C.P. before him, he enjoyed consensus management, but John did not enjoy making unpopular decisions. During his tenure, the fierce competition between the McCormick domestic sales organization and the Schilling Division did not diminish. Between visits by Bud Weiser to John's office during the day and Bob Crampton's calls to him at home at night, John could rarely relax.

One time he did relax was during the annual Grocery Manufacturers of America (GMA) meeting, which was held at the Waldorf Astoria in New York. That was the year of the famous New York blackout. It hit just as everyone was dressing for dinner. We made the most of it and spent the evening in the entertainment suite, which had been set up for greeting customers. But that night it was only McCormick people. It was a weird experience with all of New York blacked out, but fortunately our bar had been refreshed just before the blackout.

All went well until about 10:00 P.M., when a wild scream came from the corner of the darkened room. It came from John. Silence then prevailed, after which John excitedly called through the dark, "The scotch just ran out."

After the McCormick Division was formed in 1960 with Jim Welsh serving as its first General Manager, East/West meetings were set up several times a year. John thought that throwing the two groups into a hotel together was bound to solve some of their differences. And, of course, he was right.

One such meeting was held at the Seaview Country Club in New Jersey. During the meeting, John said to Ernie Issel, "Let's drive down and see what is going on." Carter Parkinson had jurisdiction over the insecticide department, which was not doing well. (For years and years it had not done well.) John quizzed Carter as to why a new competitive product called "Real Kill" was gaining 100 percent distribution and greatly outselling our own Bee Brand spray. Carter responded, "We don't worry about them. They don't even belong to the insecticide association."

During John's presidency, with C.P. remaining as Chairman, McCormick purchased Gorman Eckert in Canada (later to be renamed Club House Foods). The next year, 1961, Gilroy Foods, a processor of garlic and onion, was acquired, as was Baker Extract. Also in 1962, McCormick assumed a new dimension in real estate development with its purchase of stock in Maryland Properties, later to be fully owned and renamed McCormick Properties.

The Industrial Products Division was created in 1963 and our German company, McCormick G.m.b.H. in Frankfurt in 1964.

In 1965, Carter Parkinson succeeded Jim Welsh as Vice President and General Manager of the McCormick Division, and Harry Wells succeeded R. C. Crampton as Vice President and General Manager of the Schilling Division, which two years later moved its headquarters from San Francisco to Salinas, California.

Nineteen sixty-eight was an active year, with the acquisition of Tubed Products (then called Tubed Chemical Co.) of

Easthampton, Massachusetts and McCormick Foods (then called Childers Foods, Inc.) of Lynchburg, Virginia. In October, the corporate offices were moved nineteen miles north of Baltimore to Hunt Valley. However, C.P. remained in his beloved Light Street boardroom office and never moved to Hunt Valley. John became Chairman, and Harry Wells was elected President the next year when C.P. retired, after fifty-seven years with the Company.

Sales hit $108 million . . . C.P.'s dream goal.

We decided to buy The Hunt Valley Golf Club to augment the weekend business of The Hunt Valley Inn, which was then under construction.

Who should be picked to be responsible for the start-up of the golf? Why, of course, the low handicap golfer in the Company! This was Milt van den Berg. Milt was also the Vice President of Planning, which made additional sense for this choice.

Milt did a fine job, with one notable exception. Not being a drinking man himself, he nonetheless oversaw construction of the club bar, which turned out a little too small – would you believe *three* bar stools wide? The next year a new bar was built that extended all the way across the room.

Supply and demand!

The Hunt Valley Inn was completed in 1970 after some serious delays. The chosen site consisted of solid rock, which had to be blasted out. There were occasions when fragments of rock fell on the ninth-floor balcony of Executive Plaza I, our corporate headquarters. This was about a quarter of a mile away. The rock blasters became bolder and bolder (no pun intended) until one afternoon they blew a rock through the corner office of the Westinghouse Building, which was even farther away. Fortunately, no one was in the office at the time.

Then, came the big day when Len Gerber, President of McCormick Properties, proudly took the Corporate Board over for a walk through the nearly completed Inn. As Len walked between me and our Vice Chairman Emeritus "Pops" Luttrell, we approached the front entrance of the California-styled Inn, an unusual looking structure of dark brick without benefit of surrounding shrubbery as yet. Pops asked, "Len, did the brick have to be this color?" I don't remember there being any reply.

Brooke Furr and Grayson Luttrell catch some rest after fishing on C. P.'s boat.

When John retired, he remained as Chairman for a few years. Aside from attending Board meetings, he frequented the office only on special occasions. One such occasion was a special meeting called to review a potential acquisition of a California company. The owners of this company were young, aggressive, and successful.

The three partners arrived in town the night before and closed up Velleggia's, an Italian restaurant in Towson. At the appointed meeting hour of 9:00 A.M., they had not shown up, and John had made a special trip into the office. I called The Hunt Valley Inn, where they were staying, and woke them up. At about ten o'clock, they arrived and were invited into John's office for the meeting. Their president apologized for being late, saying, "We drank so much last night we couldn't get up." Ernie Issel stammered a little and said to the president, "Well, why don't you tell us a little about your company?" The response was "Okay," but then he choked and couldn't seem to get his mouth working right. Finally, he asked the sales manager to do it for him.

The history of the company was quite impressive. It had a California flair and was distinctly different from our McCormick culture in Baltimore.

Late in the meeting, I thought John Curlett was going to pass out. Ernie, again trying to keep the meeting on track, suggested that a good synergy would be to eliminate the California company's brokers and consolidate all sales into the McCormick Food Service sales force.

After a slight hesitation, there was a reaction from the California owner, "Noo-oo-oo, I don't think so. Brokers are good at getting the customers laid and stuff."

Well, John, who had cataracts in both his eyes, was sporting extremely thick glasses. We detected no change in his facial expression, but those glasses seemed to cloud over as if they were protecting John from hearing this.

The meeting ended abruptly.

The story has an end. We bought the company, and never could run it as well as the Californians. Years later, we sold it.

During John Curlett's years as President and then Chairman, a total of twenty-two years, Company sales grew from $39 million to $251 million. Financial returns increased, and the Company broadened its base. A Research and Development department was started with Dr. Richard Hall as its initial director, and a Home Economics department was re-created (Willoughby had a home economist in the early days).

"Fluffy" died because it cost us too much to compete (almost half our profits), but we had the dubious pleasure of knowing that we were number two in the market when we discontinued the product.

"Fun" actually blew up! The first year of testing in three markets was highly successful. I remember riding up to one of our test markets, York, Pennsylvania, with John Doub. We had been running a very creative TV spot featuring little kids riding around on big balloons, yelling and singing, "We're gonna have 'Fun.'"

Well, we walked into the first store and found the Fun display. Just then, we heard "Mommy, Mommy, there it is!" A little kid came running down the aisle and grabbed three or four packages off the display, but the mother caught up, said, "You can't have those today," and tore the packages out of the kid's clutching hands. That kid then threw one of the worst tantrums I have ever seen, going face down on the floor and kicking his legs.

I remember saying to John, "We've got it made."

We did, until the next year when we rolled the product out and got the best of our competitor, "Fizzies," in distribution. The product was being packed for us by a drug firm. To take care of our expanding volume needs, they moved to another plant with different equipment. Product from the second plant had moisture in it, and since it was effervescent, the package swelled up and would go off like a firecracker if you stepped on it.

I was sitting in a buyer's office in Tampa with Al Ireland and a broker named "Smokey" Stover. While sitting on a bench in the outer office, Smokey inadvertently put his foot down on a package of swollen Fun. It went off with a "bang." The confused Smokey exclaimed, "I didn't know it would blow!!" If conditions were right, Fun would even blow up on shelves in the store. It made a horrible mess.

Another great idea down the drain! We withdrew from the market. Dr. Dick Hall, head of Research and Development, didn't want to give up, however, quipping that our packaging only had a 40 percent sealing failure!

We had another product go bad on us that year. Our cheese dips became so hard in the foil packages that one might have tiled his shower with a few cases of the stuff. And a flavorful "good morning" to you all!

In those years, we also learned that we didn't know how to run a hotel or golf course profitably, and eventually sold them both.

Now it was Harry Wells's turn to lead the Company, which he did with great success for seventeen years.

Chapter Eight

High Growth Years – Harry Wells

A retirement party held at The Hunt Valley Inn featured Bob Sharman. At last, the Company atmosphere was going to be tranquil with Sharman gone. But he had one last zinger, and typically it was hurled at the top man. At the end of the evening, when Sharman rose to give his farewell remarks, he addressed Harry Wells. He said, "Harry, a lot of people have asked me, 'How did Harry Wells get to be President of McCormick & Company?' I always give them this answer, Harry, 'Bob Sharman chose not to run.'"

During the 1970s, Company growth was significant. When Harry was elected President in 1969, sales had just exceeded C.P.'s long-time goal of $100 million. By 1980, sales had increased to $547 million. Along with Harry's election, three others were elected as Executive Vice Presidents: Ernie Issel, Finance; Carter Parkinson, Marketing; and Clayton Shelhoss, Administration.

Harry spent a number of formative years as Plant Superintendent at the Light Street headquarters under the tutelage of Doug Reed, Vice President of Manufacturing. He then moved West as Director of Manufacturing for the Schilling Division, but he remembers some Buck Burton stories.

C.P. decided that it would save executive time if we could eliminate the fortnightly walk uptown to the barber shop. So he talked his barber, Dick Utz, into becoming the Company barber, and set up shop right off the seventh-floor lobby. To make it complete, Charlie Watts shined shoes every day after 4:00 P.M. One day, Harry and Buck

Harry Wells (left) took over the reins of leadership from John Curlett and C. P.

were sitting in the office that they shared when Charlie Watts came by and said, "Mr. Buck, you need your shoes shined?" Buck did need to have them shined. He said, "Sure," and Charlie took them away. It occurred to Harry that this might be good for a little fun, so he left the office, went next door, and called C.P. A few minutes later, Buck's phone rang. He answered and said, "Hi, Mr. C.P., how are you doing? You what? You want me to come up to your office? Damn you, how did you know I didn't have any shoes on?" C.P. loved it!

A group of us were up at the Masonic Lodge one night to watch one of our fellow employees get his third-degree initiation. Buck Burton attended for the first time in a few years and forgot the secret password. When everyone was lined up to whisper the password individually, Buck asked one of his McCormick associates for the password. His "friend" purposely whispered the wrong one in Buck's ear. So when Buck was asked for the secret word, he failed. The deacon took several steps and, in front of the crowded lodge, addressed the Grand Master. He said, "Grand Master, the word has been lost!" With that, Buck turned and in a loud voice blurted out, "You S.O.B.!"

Buck's annual highlight was the three-board (senior, junior, and factory) Christmas party held at C.P.'s house. Immediately upon arriving, Buck would drink about three "depth charges." This consisted of dropping a shot glass full of bourbon into a glass full of beer and drinking the concoction right down. Buck always tried to get others to join him in this sport, and nobody did it more than once. It was pretty lethal.

At one of these three-board parties, when Harry and Clayton Shelhoss arrived, they went right upstairs to C.P.'s closet. Each chose an expensive silk tie to wear for the party. They had a method in their madness. They suspected this would be one of those nights when C.P. would snip ties. Later, when C.P. started snipping people's ties off, he ruined two of his own favorites. Harry claims that this just about ended the tie-cutting episodes at McCormick.

With the success of the McCormick barber shop in mind, C.P. talked R.C. Crampton into creating one in San Francisco for our Schilling Division executives. With a smaller group of potential customers, the Schilling barber shop only operated a few days a week. One day, Crampton was showing off the Schilling offices to some visitors (an antique coffee house had been built to provide a feeling similar to the McCormick Tea House). As the tour passed the closed barber shop, R.C. opened the door and proudly announced that this was where his people got their haircuts. With his back to the barber chair, R.C. took a few seconds to realize that one of his employees was sleeping in it. That was the end of the Schilling barber shop.

In his early days with the Company, Harry tells us, he got a phone call from C.P.'s secretary, saying that he wanted Harry in the boardroom as fast as he could get there. The story goes like this:

I rushed up to the boardroom and arrived rather breathlessly to find C.P. literally running around the boardroom

with a fly swatter, whacking at the walls. There was a big, green, buzzing, blowfly annoying him, and he was making a major effort to do away with it. The reason for the call to me was that he wanted to let me know in no uncertain terms that there was no way I could run a food plant without having screens on the windows, and I should get them put in place as quickly as possible. I had learned by this time that you did not argue with the boss when his mind was set. You just went ahead and took care of it the best way you knew how.

I went down to the office, got a piece of paper, walked out into the middle of Light Street, and counted the windows that needed screens. This included most of the windows in the building. I arrived at a count of some one thousand screens necessary to do the job. We had just finished having screens made and installed in the salad-dressing department, so I had a reasonable idea of what they might cost. Nevertheless, I called the supplier, got an updated quote, thinking in terms of a thousand instead of the three or four that we had put in, and proceeded to write a requisition to have the job done.

Realizing that a cooling-off period is sometimes advisable, I waited until the next morning, went up to C.P.'s office, knocked on the door, and asked if I could come in. He greeted me very cordially and wanted to know what I needed. I said I had the screen thing all taken care of, and I had written a requisition to have the work done. But it was a larger amount than I was authorized to approve, and would he kindly sign the requisition. I put it on the desk. He picked it up, took one look at it, and didn't say a word for a few moments. Finally he looked up and said, "What else can we do?"

The fact is, the requisition was for $85,000, a lot of money in those days. We never did put screens in.

One of the bad habits that McCormick colleagues had was to make late-night calls when out on parties. If they were out having fun, everybody should be up having fun. Harry put a little dent in this practice one evening when he received a call from Doug Reed. Doug thought it was a great joke to tell Harry that he had received a call from the ADT Security System, and that there was a problem at the plant that Harry should go down and check out. It was two in the morning, and Harry could hear much party background noise, so he ignored the instructions. He set his alarm for six in the morning, however, and called Doug Reed, reporting that everything at the plant was okay. That was the last of the middle-of-the-night phone calls made to Harry.

Back in the late 1940s and early 1950s, each year when the National Jaycees would have their officer installation, C.P. would invite the new officers, as well as all of the delegates from the various states, to McCormick for a cocktail party and dinner. C.P. was a board member of the U.S. Chamber; Executive Vice President Jack Beane was active in the National Jaycee organization. Dinner was always held in the Tea House, and usually attended by fifty to sixty people.

According to Harry:

> I had received a call from C.P. several weeks prior to this event, and he had told me that he wanted me to be the speaker at dinner. I was totally perplexed by the request, and asked him what kind of subject I should speak on. He said whatever I thought was appropriate, which left me absolutely nowhere. I agonized over this for a long time, but finally got a speech prepared. With fear and trepidation I arrived at the dinner party that evening. As dinner concluded, C.P. got up, made a few remarks, and then introduced me as the guest speaker for the evening. Needless to say, I was scared to death. Although prepared to speak, I had absolutely no confidence that what I was going to say was relevant to anything that the group would be interested in. Nevertheless, I got up and started to speak.
>
> I had hardly gotten the first sentence out of my mouth when all hell broke loose. Directly above the Tea House, someone started hammering on the floor with an air hammer. Simultaneously, sirens broke loose from somewhere on the seventh floor, and with that, the rear windows to the Tea House opened, and six pigeons flew in. You can imagine the chaos all this caused. I had obviously been "set up," for which I was delighted, because I didn't have to give the speech. The evening was a howling success for the Jaycees, despite the fact that the pigeons made a helluva mess in the Tea House and on

some of the guests. It was great fun for everyone involved and was very much in keeping with the then very popular Broadway show, "Hellzapoppin.'" It sure did!

A much more serious function was held in the Tea House when our one and only outside director at that time, Eric Johnston, was asked to speak on the subject of his last trip to the Mideast. Four successive Presidents of the United States had used Eric for Mideast diplomacy, and his comments were always quite interesting and "off the record." This event was a lunch meeting of all the Company Boards for the purpose of hearing Eric's report. He was an eloquent speaker, and as he stood up, Bud Weiser, Vice President - Sales and Marketing, was quietly summoned to his office to take a phone message. About ten minutes later, when Eric was really into his subject and holding his audience spellbound, Bud returned, sat down at the head table, and said something to the person next to him. C.P. overheard this and said, "What?" and with that Bud proudly blurted out, "We're sold out of tea."

With this delightful but interruptive piece of information, Eric stopped in mid-sentence, while Bud elaborated on an order we had received and mentally calculated every other McCormick tea account ordering a big iced tea promotion. Well, he killed Eric's speech, because everyone in the room was now thinking what a great thing it would be to have this kind of boost in sales. This suddenly was more interesting than what the Arabs were going to do to each other on the other side of the world. Eric finished his talk but without the same fervor as before.

Unfortunately, Bud Weiser's extrapolation was just that, and come summer, we had one big warehouse full of unsold tea.

Bud was a tough sales manager, though. After he demanded that all salesmen call on at least fifty stores a week, he congratulated Don Pearson on calling on fifty-four. Pearson's retort: "I could have called on fifty-five, but some damn fool stopped to ask me what I was selling."

Years later, early in 1975, the Schilling Division decided to have a special Bicentennial pack of 4-ounce black pepper. It was determined that they would use the old "Schilling's Best" can, a dark-red-and-gold package that was the Schilling signature until the early 1950s. The product was planned to be introduced in the fall of 1975 so that it would be in the stores for the 1976 celebration. They packed 250,000 cases.

The promotion was a tremendous success. The product flew out of Schilling's warehouses. The promotion and special packaging was to last until mid-1976, but they found themselves getting low in inventory in early January. Meetings were held to determine whether to order more special cans to pack or go back to the normal Schilling can. The decision was made to produce another 100,000 cases of the Bicentennial can.

As the production Control Supervisor with forecasting responsibilities, my younger brother John McCormick found his office had become a center for sales, marketing, and operations managers dropping by to hear the latest on this great pepper sale opportunity. They were transferring product from warehouse to warehouse, and producing as packaging became available. With no experience in this type of special promotion, they really had no history to tell them how much they could sell.

One Friday morning that January, the lower left-hand corner of John's office window became the habitat for a snail. Sitting at his desk pondering the weekly sales/inventory update that he was to give for the promotion, John jokingly circled the location of the snail on the window. When he returned to work the next Monday, the snail had moved up at a 45-degree angle. He circled the location.

Since no one else could project the special pepper sales, the snail would now be John's assistant. Word spread throughout the Division, and more and more visitors stopped by. For the next four days, the snail moved up the window at roughly the same 45-degree angle, matching the sales of the pepper.

The following Monday, the snail had fallen off the window, leaving behind six linked circles up the window. John drew a vertical line from the snail's last circled position. In that morning's forecast meeting, he noted the snail's activity, but the group felt that the pepper would keep selling. Like the snail, the

Bicentennial pepper died that week! Schilling ended up with over 60,000 cases in inventory in 1978.

Nineteen seventy-six was an important decision year for McCormick. The Schilling Division was finally merged with the McCormick Division. The reconstituted Grocery Products Division had Carter Parkinson as General Manager.

For the long haul and on paper, this was a logical decision. But Harry has second-guessed the decision over the years, wondering if we might have done better to leave the Schilling Division independent. We'll never know, but I think many of us regret losing that West Coast aggressiveness and creativity that the Schilling management always displayed.

In 1976, T.V. Time and All Portions companies were acquired. The following year, Harry was honored by being elected Chairman of the National Association of Manufacturers (NAM).

Another of the human tragedies hit us in 1978 when Bob Schneider, Vice President of Manufacturing, and Stan Godwin, Vice President of Purchasing, were killed in an automobile accident while checking out an acquisition possibility in Connecticut.

All travelers have flying stories, and Harry had a most interesting travel companion on a flight from El Centro to San Francisco. It was late in May, and Harry had been helping with the mechanical harvest of onions for Gilroy Foods.

When he arrived at the small terminal building at the airport, he found a large crowd assembled, including the El Centro High School band complete with cheerleaders. They were obviously sending off some kind of celebrity, which turned out to be a frog Harry estimates to have weighed some eight pounds. When he asked the students what the occasion was, they told him that the frog was their contestant in a jumping frog contest being held in Calaveras. The frog was in a lard can, and when they took it out, Harry saw a frog with a body as large as a dinner plate, and legs that were at least a foot and a half long. When the plane arrived, the delegation from the high school and Harry Wells boarded to the cheers of the entire high school as well as the sound of the full high school marching band, playing the El Centro High fight song.

Special arrival ceremonies were made for Jack Caffey (2nd from left) by "Mayor" Paul Welsh.

Former West Coast Sales Manager Jack Caffey had a big welcome when he was flown into Baltimore for his promotion into the International Division. We had Paul Welsh, Public Relations Manager, pose as the mayor. He was accompanied by a photographer and was to greet Jack as he stepped off the plane. Our delegation was permitted to go down to the tarmac to greet Jack. What we didn't know was that Mickey Rooney was going to step off right before Caffey. Seeing the photographer and the welcoming committee, the little movie star smiled and waved, but the photographer looked right past him and flashed as Caffey stepped off the stairs into the welcoming party. Both travelers were suitably impressed.

In March of 1979, Hilly Wilson was elected President of the Company. The Harry and Hilly team directed the Company until

1987, when they both retired. And need a team we did, because in the fall of that year we were approached by the huge Swiss pharmaceutical firm Sandoz, which had decided to acquire McCormick. We fought them off for many months and became, in the "take-over" 1980s, one of the few companies successful in fighting off a large aggressor to remain independent.

Only when we sued them, and the court set up face-to-face depositions in Switzerland, did we get an offer from them to go away. We paid a little "green mail" in order to end the litigation, which was sapping our strength. I remember I was appalled at the thought of giving them any profit on any of the stock they had acquired. I felt we should let them get out the same way they got in. But our lawyers and bankers felt that we had won and should get it over with as promptly as possible.

I had a dream the night before the special Board meeting that netted the agreement. The dream was one of those very clear, seemingly realistic ones. It seems that we had told Sandoz to send their fittest young executives over for a touch football game to be played across the street from our headquarters at Executive Plaza I. The outcome of the game would determine whether McCormick would remain an independent company.

The Sandoz team arrived, and our Multiple Management Board members went out and beat the hell out of them. It was that kind of indignation and confidence I believe we all felt under Harry's strong leadership during those trying Sandoz days.

During this same period, Dave Haukedalen, Director of Planning, and I attended a management seminar. At one of the sessions, a Sandoz executive from their North American division saw Dave's name tag and came over to him, saying, "You should not worry about Sandoz taking you over. They let us run our U.S. division without interference." But oddly enough, the gentleman's Swiss accent was so strong, Dave could hardly understand him.

One of our all time characters was Howard Auerswald. Howard founded Tubed Products and ran it after it was acquired by McCormick. Howard loved to play golf and laughed his way around most courses. But underneath all the humor, he was quite competitive and liked to win. He created many versions of betting to fit whatever skills or weaknesses his opponents might have.

Auerswald always got pretty charged up for the annual management meetings that we had at Seaview, New Jersey, since he enjoyed them so much. But one year he was beside himself. His good friend John Gill, President of our Club House Foods in Canada, had arranged his own transportation from London, Ontario to Seaview by using the Company plane. This was a real time-saver between those two spots. Howard asked John if he would mind stopping off at Springfield, Massachusetts, since it was right on his way, to pick him up and give him a ride.

John said, "Fine, but I'll see that you get charged for half of the flight." Howard said, "Why? You're not incurring any expense; just land and pick me up." John said, "No way. Pay or you don't go." Howard was furious and arrived via other transportation. What really blew his mind came at the end of the meetings. We were all standing in front of the hotel, getting our cars for the ride home, when a big, long, black limousine arrived to take John to the Seaview airport for his lonely airplane ride home.

Auerswald, like any good competitor, won some and lost some. He had been anxious to do business with Mary Kay Cosmetics for many years, but had had little success. He finally arranged a dinner in Dallas with a small group, and made sure to have Mary Kay's Executive Vice President at his side. Howard was elated, and went into his best joke- and story-telling mode, at which he was greatly skilled. He had the whole table laughing, even the elusive customer. Howard turned on the full charm and addressed the next joke directly to his prey. The table exploded with laughter. In an act of familiarity and amid much laughter on his own part, Howard accidently brought his hand down and slapped his new friend on the knee.

All hell broke loose. The customer yelled, "What the hell do you think you're doing?" and pushed his chair away from Howard's. All the smiles turned sour, and the hunt for new sales was over.

PEPPER PEOPLE

After Hilly Wilson became President, he initiated a quarterly meeting of the operating executives. Most of these were held in Hunt Valley, and Hilly liked to go to Shane's Restaurant for dinner. Some of the group didn't particularly like Shane's, but it was close to our offices and The Hunt Valley Inn, where the out-of-town executives stayed. Hilly's drink was always Jack Daniels, and he was most particular about how much of it was poured over the rocks.

On our last trip to Shane's, Jack Felton, Vice President of Corporate Communications, suggested that it would be practical to let the thirty people attending order beef or fish, but limit the menu to two items for the main course. Hilly didn't like that idea and said, "No, just let everyone order what they want." Few kitchens are equipped to serve thirty orders of different items all at the same time. Shane's did the best they could, but it became a disaster because, as Jack Felton expected, the orders got all mixed up.

Hilly was really not concerned about this confusion until Felton asked a harried waitress to stop what she was doing and bring Hilly a refill of Jack Daniels. When it arrived with half a lime squeezed into it, Hilly saw the light. We never returned to Shane's.

Hilly was great one night in Atlantic City, however. We were holding a "pepper putt" golf tournament at Seaview, which Milt van den Berg had arranged for a number of years. This was a non-Company event, but all contestants were "pepper" people. Milt always won, but a good time was had by all. On one particular night, most of the group went into Atlantic City. We arrived at a local watering hole (there were probably a dozen or so of us). Rather early on, several of us were propositioned by some of the working girls. As a joke, we told them that they would have to negotiate a group rate with our lawyer, who at that time was none other than Hilly.

When they found out Hilly was a widower, one of these girls got Hilly aside and went after him like an Electrolux vacuum-cleaner salesperson. Hilly knew he'd been set up and thought it was funny. They talked and negotiated and argued and compromised and talked some more. Finally, after half an hour, the woman looked happy and came over to announce to all of us that a rate had finally been set. Hilly walked up behind her grinning from ear to ear. She named the small amount, which I've forgotten, and said, "Hilly has agreed to this rate for each of you." Hilly interrupted her and yelled, "No, no, that's not each, that's for the whole group!" The room collapsed in laughter, and we thought the lady was going to kill him before she stomped out of the room. You never can trust those lawyers!

One year, Harry and Hilly went to a financial analyst meeting at the University Club in New York. It was the end of a long week of analyst meetings held in Dallas, Houston, Los Angeles, San Francisco, Chicago, Boston, and Hartford. New York was the final one, and everyone was tired, especially Harry, who didn't like these meetings much anyway.

Jack Felton remembers the following story:

> We were in the meeting room where Harry was to speak. I was adjusting the podium to fit Harry's new bifocals, when I asked him if he would like something to drink. The analysts were already in the next room having cocktails. Harry said, "Just some plain tomato juice, please." I told the waiter, who came back with a huge glass of tomato juice and put it on the podium in such a way that it spilled all down the front of Harry's trousers. He was wearing a light summer suit. We were just twenty minutes from the start of Harry's presentation, so I told the waiter to get some towels, fast. We wiped off all the tomato juice we could, and I asked the waiter to find a hair dryer. He came back with one, and off Harry went to the men's room to dry his pants. Just about then, Hilly came in and said, "Where's Harry?" I said, "He'll be back in a minute." Hilly said, "Where is he? He should be in there shaking hands with the analysts." He kept on asking where Harry was and I finally said, "He's in the men's room." Hilly said, "What's he doing in there?" I said, "Hilly, he's blow-drying his pants." Hilly just shook his head, took another big swig of his Jack Daniels, and went back into the other room.

There were two sizeable acquisitions in 1981 – Stange and Setco.

But business in the '80s wasn't keeping pace with the '70s. Real estate gains from property sales distorted our profit comparisons.

According to Dave Haukedalen, who was Director of Corporate Planning at that time, some felt that the McCormick ship of state was "becalmed." A high-level committee was formed to focus on important research projects that would merit corporate funding. The committee included President Hilly Wilson, Dr. Dick Hall, Don Dick, Bailey Thomas, Gordon Yates, and Dave.

The first few meetings didn't seem to get much past the name and charter of the committee (the name SRDRC). You guess the full name; I can't remember. At some point, it was suggested that the committee should include some "creative" operating people. Aha! Who better than Frank Skeans, who was indeed creative and an operating person. Also, Frank was new to the Company, having been recently installed as General Manager of the Food Service Division. Skeans had served as Executive Vice President of Stange prior to our acquisition. I quote Haukedalen:

> I'll never forget Frank's first (and last) contribution to the deliberations of the committee. Impatient as he was, Frank suffered through some pontifications laced with platitudes like: leading edge, competitive edge, forefront, strategic, recombinant DNA, gene splicing, etc. Abruptly, Frank stood up, folded his arms and strode to the front of the table. He then advised something like the following: "What the #!!@!! is this committee all about? I thought we would be watching trends and charting our course. What we should make, what should we get out of, etc. etc." The rest of the speech is probably best not repeated, but in harsh terms, he ended up suggesting that we really should determine where we were going and how should we get there.
>
> Gordon Yates paled and stared at the ceiling. Dr. Hall smiled and inspected his shoes. Hilly went harrrmmmppphhh, and Haukedalen, the corporate planner, worried about how to properly record the suggestion in the minutes of the meeting. Bailey, by the way, frequently spent his time at such meetings by reading his mail and jotting down notes to his secretary.

We all sometimes say the wrong thing. We always give a gift of products to shareholders attending our Annual Meeting. When Hilly was Corporate Secretary of the Company, it was a tradition that he announce the Company gift to shareholders at the end of the Annual Meeting. One year, instead of pronouncing "hors d'oeuvres" properly, he shocked the audience by saying, "This new product is especially nice for 'whore's ovaries.'" You can't imagine the look on the shareholders' faces.

There's an old joke about the guy who got left field so fouled up, nobody could play it. Well, a few years later at the shareholders' meeting, Jim Harrison was Corporate Secretary. Having heard Hilly needled for years about his gaffe, Jim was concerned because he was announcing our gift of a mix to make French "crêpes." Our home economists were using the French pronunciation "crepps." Jim wanted to use the right French pronunciation, but when he stood up in front of the McCormick shareholders, he announced our new product was "creative craps." At first shareholders were stunned; then they howled.

Even Corporate Communications' expert Jack Felton can falter. On a radio talk show in the U.K., doing a little public relations for our Schwartz brand, Jack was introduced as a world expert on spices. After some polite comments about how nice it was to be in Northern England, Jack talked a little about spice usage around the world. Then the telephone rang. The first lady to call was a very elegant-sounding English lady. While on the air, she said she had two chicken breasts and wondered how she should season them. Her question to Jack was: "So what do I do with my breasts?" Jack answered by telling this proper English lady she should sauté her breasts in butter and garlic, cover them with nutmeg and cream, and pop them in the oven. Meanwhile, the talk show host was so doubled up with laughter that he couldn't talk and could hardly take the next call.

But Jack was good, too. This is his own story:

> After the first few days of the Sandoz takeover crisis, I went into Harry Wells and said, "We need to make some kind of statement about where we are in this whole situation." All of us had been sitting around for days while very expensive

investment bankers kept telling us all the things we couldn't do and none of the things we could do. Harry said, "Jack, you're right." I went to Don Dick, who was Treasurer at the time, and said, "Don, we need to get on with the things we can do and I need a quote for the Wall Street Journal and the other papers." Don said, "You're right." So the next day during another long meeting, with all the outside advisors again telling us what we couldn't do, I finally said, "I need to know what we can do and I'm ready to fight! I need some quotes for the news media. I can't stall them any longer." Harry and Don both said, "Jack's right." As a result, we quickly got some quotes together, and we had a statement.

While I was giving our statement to Tim Metz at the *Wall Street Journal*, he said, "Jack, the Sandoz people keep telling me they are friendly. How friendly are they?" I said, "I think they are about as friendly as circling sharks." Of course that was the quote that ended up the next day in the *Wall Street Journal*. We thought it was funny. The head guy from Sandoz U.S. called Harry to complain about the unfair tactics we were using in fighting their "friendly takeover offer." Swiss officials rarely talk to the press, so we used similar tactics in continuing to fight off Sandoz. Finally, even the Swiss press began to ask Sandoz officials who was giving them such bad advice on their takeover tactics. The Swiss press even did a cartoon showing a Sandoz executive with too much pepper up his nose and the tag line that McCormick was too hot to handle, and nothing to sneeze at!

Harry liked golf, but I have seen him on several occasions carry his golf beyond the course.

Once, at the Country Club of Maryland, Harry sliced his drive on the ninth hole. The ball went out into the road just as a poor fellow was driving along in a station wagon. It bounced into the driver's door and the car abruptly halted. The driver got out and inspected the damage. While he was doing this, Harry put a second ball down, and hit it in exactly the same place. This shot took one bounce and hit the back door about a foot away from the driver's head. The frightened motorist jumped back into the car without ever looking back and, in a cloud of dust with spinning wheels, took off down the road.

Some years later in California, Harry inflicted more car damage. We had just finished playing his home course at Green Hills and walked up to the parking lot. Harry had a new Thunderbird, one of the first, the most beautiful powder blue convertible you have ever seen. Next to it was another car, the right-hand door of which had been opened so carelessly that it had put a big mark down the side of Harry's new driver-side door. I wanted to cry, but stoic Harry said nothing. He merely got into his car, drove it forward several car lengths, stopped, and got out. He then walked to the other car and, with a swift kick, stomped the door in. Still saying nothing, he drove home.

Every team, every company, every organization needs balance. One of our balances was Gordon Yates. Harry had much admiration for Gordon's abilities from their days at Schilling, and Gordon moved to Baltimore and became Vice President - Administration. I always enjoyed my reporting relationship with Gordon, because we were real opposites. At the same time, we liked and respected each other.

I can best describe Gordon as a military by-the-book man. He was a graduate of the Merchant Marine Academy. To Gordon, there is only one way to do something, and that's the way the manual tells you to do it.

To Gordon, the secret to success was proper organization and proper regulations. So Gordon completed the very difficult job of supervising the writing of Company Policies and Procedures. Now we'll agree that a company of our size needs a certain number of policies and procedures. Most of us just don't like to write them. But when Gordon published a "policy on procedures" and a "procedure on policies," I thought he'd gone overboard. That is, until Gordon carefully explained to me why it was necessary in a most convincing manner.

While in Boston with our Secretary and General Counsel, Dick Single, doing business for Tubed Products, Gordon and Dick went to the popular Anthony's Pier 4 seafood restaurant. They were told they would have to wait twenty-five minutes for a table, and

Gordon suggested that that gave them just enough time for two drinks. Gordon always prided himself on planning all his time carefully.

When they finished their two drinks Dick suggested another. But Gordon looked at his watch and said, "The table should be ready." Just as Gordon paid the check, the loudspeaker said, "Mr. Yates, your table is ready."

Dick was quite impressed with this display of "organization at work!"

And for those of you who may not know that Harry Wells was also a salesman, read this as told by Harry:

> As part of my exposure to the Schilling sales organization, and to Schilling's good customers, I was sent on a sales trip to Alaska. Schilling had many, many good customers in Alaska, and this sales trip was not only interesting, but certainly productive in terms of the Company's business. One of the highlights of the trip, however, was the Saturday morning call in Juneau, Alaska. The call was by previous appointment and was on the Territorial Prison, a very good Schilling customer for all of our spices, as well as coffee and tea.
>
> I arrived at the prison at the appointed time, went through the necessary security checks, and was ushered into the food-service area of the facility. I was told the buyer had a small office at the end of the cafeteria, which I located, and went in and introduced myself. You can imagine my surprise when I found the man I was going to be selling was in a black-and-white-striped suite — big, black-and-white stripes, in fact. He was an inmate! It was a great morning, however, because Schilling got a huge order for the spices they needed plus a tremendous order for Schilling coffee.
>
> The second-most interesting part of the trip and one that is probably unique among McCormick salespeople was a call made on an Indian trading post situated on an island near Sitka. To make this call, it was necessary to rent a rowboat and row out to the island in order to contact the buyer. Again, Schilling got a huge order for all of the spices as well as coffee, and I had an experience that I am sure few McCormick salesmen would have ever had: a "Hertz Rent-A-Boat."

In the early 1970s, market research told us that our competitor, Spice Islands, was perceived somewhat differently from our own gourmet brand. Spice Islands had only one package. It had originally been introduced through specialty and department stores before moving into the supermarkets. It also carried the highest prices of any spice line. Our gourmet line, while viewed as being beautifully packaged and with high product quality, was perceived as just another brand of McCormick, the biggest in the business. It was difficult to assume that we could ever completely conquer that small niche market of consumers looking for a little snob appeal or looking for a kitchen display brand "different" from their neighbor's.

Therefore, we decided to create yet another brand of gourmet spices. This one was to be sold to specialty stores and department stores for a few years and, if successful, to be rolled out later into supermarket distribution.

We brought aboard a talented department-store marketing executive named Ann Travelstead to head up sales and marketing. We named our new line "5th Season," and it included a full line of spices, special display combinations of six-packs of spices, and unique line of tea packed in colorful vacuum-packed cans.

Ann developed a wonderful marketing program we needed to introduce the line. The largest retail outlet for gourmet foods was the prestigious headquarters of Bloomingdale's in New York City. Ann got the buyer's name from a friend and was told that he was tough to even get an appointment with, much less sell. She called him on the phone and invited him to lunch, saying that she had a new line to introduce, that she heard that he was the toughest buyer in the United States, and that she wanted to sell him before anyone else.

Ann found out he liked martinis and at lunch introduced the buyer to our new 5th Season drink recipe – a "peppertini"! A peppertini is a martini with the olive replaced by green peppercorns. Well, this "selling of the steak by its sizzle" worked. The buyer thought the peppertinis, of which he had quite a few before and during lunch, were terrific! He bought the whole line for all the Bloomingdale stores and thus 5th Season was launched.

In the second year of 5th Season sales, we decided to add bottled spring water to the line. These waters were just becoming popular in specialty stores and had not yet been promoted to the general public. We had a source of spring water right in Baltimore County and couldn't wait to introduce a product with zero product cost. The "Sales Prevention Committee" won again. Our labs told us that a chemical reaction could take place between natural water and glass, thereby limiting the product's shelf life. Someone forgot to tell Perrier. Another great idea down the tubes!

Three years later, we test-marketed in supermarkets 5th Season versus our regular Gourmet. It was a draw, and we decided to stick with Gourmet and discontinue the small-volume 5th Season line.

After the Setco acquisition in 1981, things at that subsidiary went smoothly for a few months. Setco was the business segment leader in providing small plastic bottles to the vitamin industry. Spice companies were converting many packages to plastic. Setco was also marketing to the cosmetic industry, which was also converting to plastic.

The owners of Setco were Tom and Doris Segar. Tom continued as President of Setco after the McCormick acquisition. Tom's father had created the cartoon "Popeye," and Tom was the model for Swee'pea.

Six months after the acquisition, however, Tom Segar had a few heart problems. His doctor advised him to retire. My wife, Jimi, and I moved to Los Angeles for three to six months, for me to replace Tom as President of Setco. However, the roof didn't wait for me to settle before caving in. Setco lost money for the next thirteen months. Our three- to six-month temporary stay turned into five and a half action-packed years!

Tom Segar was "California" all the way. One day, as he was roller skating to Culver City to go to work, a skate broke, throwing Tom into the gutter. His secretary was summoned to pick him up. Her description of her boss sitting on a curb with blood running down his leg, holding a pair of broken roller skates, was picturesque. About that time, Setco was really beating on its competition, and this was a business doubling in sales every year. To retaliate, competitors spread the word that Setco was in financial difficulty.

Tom solved two problems at once by improving his mode of transportation and shutting up the competitors. For himself he bought the fanciest Porsche available, the 928. He had trouble buying it because he was dressed almost as casually as a bum, and the salesman didn't want to waste time showing him the car. So Tom decided to show that salesman a thing or two. He ordered Porsche 924's for the entire sales force. That shut up the competitors! That worked fine until McCormick arrived. Every six months or so, Hilly Wilson, then President, would call me to say that Tom Miller, Vice President - Purchasing, had reminded him again that Setco was not conforming to the Company automobile policy. That problem was quite low on my priority list at the time, since we were trying to keep our people motivated during a very tough turnaround.

We got rid of the Porsches as the leases ran out, and downgraded to Datsun 280Z's. Pretty nifty cars, but a first step toward conforming to Corporate policy.

Harry Wells came to California to visit our old Culver City plant. We were delighted to see Harry and wanted his trip to be pleasant. There was one Porsche left, and that belonged to Setco Vice President - Sales and Marketing Jeff Segar, Tom's son. I asked Jeff to leave the Porsche at home during Harry's visit, and instructed that all Company 280Z's and 300Z's be parked around the side of the building.

When Harry arrived, the parking slots in front of the building were filled with a mishmash of rusty trucks and cars, and Jeff's wife's old Volkswagen camper.

After a careful plant tour, I blew it all with the transportation plans for lunch. I suggested that Harry ride with our new Vice President, Harvey Casey, so that they could get to know one another. Harvey turned all red, started to sweat, and then led Harry around the side of the building, where about eight or nine brand-new Datsuns were lined up. It looked like a California dealer's showroom.

Harry just laughed and never said a word.

The next time he visited, it was even worse. We had moved and built a beautiful plant in Anaheim. We had also acquired Poly-Vue Plastics. The president of Poly-Vue, George Grosshans, joined Setco for a while. George had leased a new Jaguar just before the acquisition and was allowed to keep the car until his lease ran out. Would you believe, I made the same mistake all over again, this time suggesting that Harry ride to lunch with George Grosshans! Harry said to George, "Nice car," and turned to give me another of his big smiles.

That night, about ten of us went to dinner. Harry insisted that he was going to pay the check. Harvey Casey asked Harry if he would like some white wine. Harry said, "Sure," and Harvey ordered the wine. Harvey then asked Harry if he would like some red wine. Harry said, "No thanks," but Harvey ordered a few expensive bottles of Jordan Cabernet Sauvignon anyway. After a wonderful dinner, Harvey asked Harry if he would like some chocolate-covered strawberries. Harry replied, "No, thank you." Harvey said, "You really have to try one, they're outstanding." With that, Harvey ordered something from the waiter, and amid coffee, this *huge* platter of chocolate-covered strawberries was placed in the center of the table. Great big beautiful chocolate-covered strawberries. Harvey says to Harry, "These are really great." Finally feeling a little indignant, Harry says, "For what I'm sure they cost, they should be." Sitting next to Harvey, I whispered, "Have you ever heard of the Last Supper? If Harry gets this bill, it will most certainly be your last!" You have never seen a three-hundred-pound man so speedily, yet quietly, eject himself out of a dinner chair as Harvey did. Harry never saw that check, and Setco was saved for another day.

Another day was actually an evening at a drug and vitamin convention in Palm Springs, California. It was very late when Jeff Segar said to Don Parodi, Director of Sales, "We need to do something outstanding to get a little recognition from this customer group."

Don Parodi's wife was awakened when Don came into the bedroom at 2:15 A.M., picked up the phone, and asked room service to deliver one hundred Bloody Marys at ten o'clock the next morning. At precisely ten o'clock the next morning, the meeting chairman announced, "Our friends at Setco are providing a 'California Coffee Break.' Bloody Marys are awaiting you in the corridor." A standing ovation occurred, followed by mass tramping out the doors. The crowd didn't return for forty-five minutes, and even then arrived carrying refills of the red stuff. Jeff Segar and I were amazed at our success, and Don Parodi just smiled in reflection of his genius.

"California coffee breaks" by Setco remain an annual event.

Over at Golden West Foods, another of our small but fast-growing units, Paul Irwin was building new business prior to his appointment as General Manager of the larger Food Service Division, and eventually General Manager of our largest division, the McCormick/Schilling Division.

Paul tells us another dinner story:

> Back in the early days of Golden West Foods, I had the pleasure of being the start-up General Manager in Gilroy, California. We assembled a project team dedicated to manufacturing, marketing, and sales for this young division. After struggling for over thirteen months, we finally produced a month with a real, legitimate operating profit. After three months in a row, I felt it was time to take this group out for dinner to celebrate the occasion. This coincided with an American Frozen Food Institute convention in San Francisco, and six of our managers and their wives were invited to attend this convention and go to dinner at the l'Etoile Restaurant in the Huntington Hotel on Nob Hill, a very elegant San Francisco restaurant.
>
> Before we went to the restaurant, I noticed that several members of our party were decked out in leisure suits and open shirts with no ties. We quickly rushed around, got appropriate neckties, and fixed up their appearance for this special continental dinner. Then off we went, a happy group, to the l'Etoile. This was certainly a most elegant French restaurant with impeccable service and outstanding food. After having drinks in the cocktail lounge, we were seated at two tables of six, and I advised the maitre d' to provide a bottle of wine for each table.
>
> The evening went along quite well and, after several courses, I noticed everyone seemed to be having plenty of wine to drink. But we had never ordered another bottle, nor had the waiter brought new bottles to our tables. As was the custom at l'Etoile, wine was placed in elevated buckets at table height. It was easy for the customers to reach over and pour from the bottle, as opposed to having the waiter do the pouring, if they felt so inclined. It turned out that many of the other patrons of the restaurant had also ordered bottles of wine. In the enthusiasm of the evening, members of our group, assuming all the wine was ours, simply reached over and grabbed any bottle that happened to be nearby and

poured wine around the table. Our check was for only two bottles, and what was even more interesting was that none of the neighboring customers seemed to notice that our group had consumed six or seven bottles of their wine during the course of this lovely dinner. The maitre d' thanked us profusely for our patronage, and all the surrounding patrons waved a friendly farewell as we left.

As McCormick Properties continued to expand, Shawan Center was developed across the street from our Hunt Valley headquarters. The Indian word "shawan" means "hunting ground." Jack Felton decided that for the opening of this new park, we should use Indians from the Chesapeake area as dancers and for a special Indian dedication ceremony. The morning of the dedication, the Indian medicine man arrived early, beautifully dressed in a white feather costume; but he was far too drunk to lead the ceremonies in front of all the news media, invited guests, and dignitaries. We quickly substituted an Indian princess for the press ceremonies while the medicine man was persuaded to sleep off his booze in a nearby trailer.

Felton also warned Len Gerber, head of McCormick Properties, that the Indians might ask him to join them in a dedication dance. Shy Len said, "I won't do it!" Sure enough, as the final dance started, the Indian children first asked the county officials and then Len to join in the dance. Under the circumstances, Len could hardly refuse. Next morning in the center of the business page of the Baltimore Sun was a picture of Len dancing with the Indians. The next day, Felton sent Gerber a copy of the old Ginger Rogers/Fred Astaire recording, "I Won't Dance . . . Don't Ask Me."

Many years before, there was another occasion when Len Gerber was made to dance. Len was a very serious young man, a quiet accountant, and a bachelor at the time. Our Treasurer, Ernie Issel, told me that he was sending Len down to Florida for a few days in the sun. Ernie said, "Buzz, see to it that Len has some fun while he's down there." Another employee, Keene Roadman, and I, together with our families, had been vacationing for a week in Daytona Beach when Len arrived. It was a Saturday evening, and a show was taking place in the hotel ballroom. We had arranged a date for Len. All this was unknown to Len, but done in his behalf. As he arrived at the hotel, he had a message to join us immediately in the ballroom. As he peeked into the room, Roadman met him and escorted him across the room to a table set for two. Sitting there was a gorgeous radio personality whom we had met the night before. She was wearing a bright red silk dress with short sleeves and long white gloves. She was exquisite. Len was forced to dance. For the next few days, we introduced Len to every pretty girl who came within shouting distance of the hotel or its beach.

Our efforts were rewarded several days later when we were walking down the street with Len. A convertible full of pretty girls passed, screeched on the brakes, and yelled to Len to join them. Our shy Len ran to the curb, vaulted into the convertible's back seat, and sped off in the car. Roadman and I watched flabbergasted.

On a more serious mission, Len was called into the Corporate Board meeting after he had spent some time in Italy reviewing the poor financial results from an ill-timed Italian venture. Bud Weiser had been responsible for our market entrance there, and we were beginning to lose significant money. In the boardroom, after Bud made some erroneous statements about the market, Len made his now-famous statement: "Bud, you can't understand the Italian marketplace by looking at it through Cadillac windows." Vice President Weiser was stunned, and a long silence followed. The grapevine very swiftly carried this apt quote into the Tea House, and Len became an instant hero. Len did, however, have enough sense to stay away from the boardroom for quite a while.

Jack Thompson, Vice President-Management Information Systems, still talks about his original job interview in 1971:

> Bob McFadden and Jack Buckley took a trip to New York City to interview prospective candidates for a computer whiz to direct the corporate information system. Both Bob and Jack had a tiring morning and went to lunch. I happened to be the first candidate interviewed after lunch. It was a nice sunny day, and Jack Buckley and Bob were sitting across from me,

with the sun shining in on Jack. I was going through my bag of tricks when I noticed that Jack Buckley was nodding and then fell fast asleep. As if that wasn't bad enough, he then began to snore. I went through my background and experience rather quickly, packed up my bag, and left. I figured I'd never see them again, and was quite surprised to receive a call and eventually be hired based on that luncheon experience. Over the years, Jack denied this vehemently, but on just as many occasions, Bob McFadden substantiated my observations.

Bob McFadden tells about another interview experience. This story is about Ernie Issel:

> I was shepherding a prospective management trainee around one afternoon. We had met with several of our senior executives already, and I was quite impressed with this applicant's poise and the manner in which he had answered some difficult questions posed to him by Carter Parkinson, Clayton Shelhoss, and others. The applicant was a decorated infantry captain in Vietnam and a Dartmouth undergraduate, and he later earned an MBA from Columbia. He was also active in a wide variety of extracurricular activities. He was well dressed and knew what he wanted to do. He knew he was interviewing well and was quite self-confident. I ushered him into Ernie's office and introduced them to each other. Ernie took the application and rumbled that he wanted to review it before beginning the interview. He studied it and then studied it some more. It seemed like forever.
>
> The silence was a bit nerve-racking, and I could see the applicant beginning to fidget as he tried to anticipate what questions he would be asked by this big, imposing, stern-faced man. Finally, Ernie put down the application.
>
> He had noted under extracurricular activities that the applicant had been President of the Black Widow Society. The applicant braced himself for some tough question about the quality of his thinking regarding his career or some similar question, and Ernie said, "Tell me about the Black Widow Society." The applicant's mind went blank. He couldn't remember what it was. He completely lost his poise because of this unexpected question. Ernie, humanely, moved on to a

more expected line of questioning. Big Ernie, a former wrestler from Lehigh, could be disconcerting.

Bob continues with another story about Ernie:

I had an encounter with Ernie Issel when he was Chairman of the Compensation Committee, and I was the newly appointed Secretary to the committee. Ernie was diligent in telling me about details that I needed to master – things such as, "Always put the date and initials of the author on graphs and charts, etc." Several months later, Ernie sat me down to review my progress. He was very open and really wanted to help me. However, his list of needed improvements was long! I listened and squirmed uncomfortably and wanted the discussion to end. But he went on and on. It seemed to me that he had covered everything already. Finally, he paused, and I took advantage of his pause by leaping to my feet and explaining that I welcomed his input and that I had to go to another meeting.

I rushed from his office and around the boardroom to go to Gordon Yates's office. As I left, I heard Ernie tell his secretary, Gerry Campbell, to find me and bring me back to have a slice of his birthday cake with him.

A few minutes later, Gerry found me in Gordon's office and gave me the message. I said, "Gerry, tell him you can't find me." At that moment, I didn't think I would enjoy sharing his birthday cake, as I was still smarting from his critique of my work. Gerry responded by saying, "Bob, go have a piece of that g— d— birthday cake so that I can get back to my work." Now I had been chewed out twice! The birthday cake somehow lacked good flavor, it seemed to me.

I have another Ernie Issel story which took place in New York City. Ernie and I were attending a seminar together and took in one of the local restaurants for dinner. Afterward, we went to the Place Elegante, a favorite restaurant and piano bar frequented by members of the spice industry.

Time flew and at two in the morning, the place closed and we were out on the street. We hailed a cab and Ernie asked the driver where we should go. The taxi driver told us that all restaurants and bars were required to close at 2:00 A.M., and that nothing was open except clubs. Ernie then directed him to take us to a club. The driver explained that we would not be permitted to enter the club, but Ernie said, "Don't worry, we'll get in."

We pulled up to a gated building on 54th Street several blocks away from the Place Elegante, and paid the cab fare. At that point, we were confronted by a uniformed guard who wanted to see our membership card. Ernie said, "I am a member of the Baltimore Country Club, and we have reciprocal rights." The guard said, "No, there are no reciprocal rights with this club." Ernie said, "You don't know what you're talking about; we have reciprocal rights."

The argument continued for a couple of more rounds. Then all of a sudden, I saw a quick movement of Ernie's fist and the guard went down like a sack of potatoes. Ernie yelled, "Run, Buzz," and we took off down the long block to the corner and hailed a passing cab. Out of breath, we both laughed all the way back to the Roosevelt Hotel.

Through the years the Multiple Management Board system has provided the necessary framework to achieve the continuity of the people philosophy that has made McCormick so successful since the 1930s.

Middle-management managers serving on "MM" boards have their eyes opened to the many other areas of the Company aside from their own specialty. They become proficient in interacting with others, in respecting other points of view, in making presentations, and in contributing group ideas to improve the Company.

The members work extremely hard at these Board activities in addition to their regular responsibilities. Over the years, many of them have played hard also. Many of their shenanigans are sprinkled through this book, but here are several more.

Joe Wertzberger provides a sense of what can happen when a group of Sales Board members get together. Joe had just hosted a committee meeting of the Sales Board:

> **In the early '70s, my wife Janie, who was my fiancée at the time, and I went to breakfast with two other McCormick**

couples. We had all partied heavily the night before and decided we needed something in our stomachs other than scotch. Someone suggested the famous omelet house nearby, which we often frequented. It was the home of 100 different omelets and very good.

As usual, when we arrived it was packed. A typical Saturday morning meant at least a thirty-minute wait, but a nice lounge outside on a beautiful day in Los Angeles made the wait tolerable. One Bloody Mary led to the next and on top of everything the night before, it didn't take me long to feel loose again.

After twenty minutes went by, one associate asked if I had left my name on the waiting list. I replied that I thought he had. To make a long story short, neither of us had, and I said I'd take care of it. All alone, I sauntered up to the lovely young hostess behind the podium with the long waiting list. She couldn't have been more than twenty years old and was new. Like always, she asked for my name.

Now, the unusual thing I instantly remembered about this place was that for some reason, they paged all parties by both their first and last names. For example, it was never "Wertzberger, party of six." It was "*Joe* Wertzberger, party of six."

So, in a joking mood, when she asked my name I went into my best Texas accent and replied, "Arted." As she wrote she responded, "First name please, Mr. Arted?" Still in my best Southern drawl, I said, "Well little lady, I'm in the horse business in Texas and go by a nickname. . . . Everyone just calls me 'Hoof.'"

I walked away and waited with our group for another fifteen minutes or so, when very loud and clear over the P.A. both inside and out, was announced, "HOOF ARTED . . . HOOF ARTED, party of six." Janie looked at me like she wanted to kill. As we sheepishly made our way to the hostess, everyone in the outside lounge was enjoying a great laugh. Even waitresses were giggling. I guess we were not fast enough, because again this modest young hostess announced "HOOF ARTED!" Some guy yelled from behind us, "It wasn't me!" From my left, a waitress, laughing uncontrollably, ran to the podium yelling, "Stop it, please!"

She whispered to the hostess, who then threw both hands

over her mouth as if in an attempt to take everything back, but it was too late. As our group followed her inside, the place was loud with laughter. Several people stood up and gave us a round of applause, honest. Even the young hostess finally smiled ear to ear and in a bright red face said she had royally been initiated into her new job.

Oh yeah, Janie waited outside for quite awhile before joining us, but she married me later anyway, so it couldn't have been all that bad. Just a typical day, she would later learn, for three McCormick couples out on the town together.

When Jack Thompson was Chairman of the Corporate Multiple Management Board, he scheduled a social outing ("outing" in this case meaning "outside"). Here's Jack:

We decided on a trip down the Gunpowder River as the social highlight of the year. We rented a big truck, piled the inner tubes and platforms into the truck, and took off. We had wine and beer and fast-food chicken. We put the beer and wine in plastic cases and floated them in the inner tubes, and put all the boxes of chicken on one of the rafts. I can still see us pushing off one by one and two by two into the fog out on the Gunpowder River. Dick Single was in charge of the wine. Don Clark was in charge of the beer, and I was the chicken man.

We miscalculated because they had just opened up the dam, and the water was flowing swiftly and was freezing cold. We had a couple of people abandon the trip because they couldn't stand the cold. Dick Single lost the wine in the bottom of the Gunpowder River, Don Clark threw a beer to somebody else and broke open Bill Galletto's mouth, and some people got tangled up in some of the trees that had fallen down the embankment. In the course of trying to fix up Bill Galletto's lip, I lost the key to my car in the mud, with no way to call home to have someone come and get me. One of the fellows with us had his inner tube spring a leak, and he sank into the water. He claims to this day that we did it on purpose. Those of us who survived piled back into the truck and showed up at my house looking like something that just arrived from a Vietnam border patrol.

If you're not afraid to read another Joe Wertzberger story, here it is:

The first time I laid eyes upon my now good friend Dave Kuhns was at the first-ever combined McCormick/Schilling Sales Board meeting in 1976. This was an historic occasion as East met West after the recent consolidation, and the seating arrangements told the whole story: Schilling members on one side of the table and McCormick members on the other. It looked like the Hatfields and McCoys. We might be joined on paper but not in spirit.

We, from Schilling, were soon told by R.J. Crampton, Director of Sales for McCormick, that the first half day of the meeting had to be devoted to closing out the former McCormick Board by way of finalizing a few Eastern projects in progress. We from the West had a right to listen, but not to vote.

I was then a young, impressionable twenty-seven year old at my first ever Board meeting and did not know what to expect. One thing I was sure of at the time, however, was that I was about to witness an extremely professional and businesslike session. After all, this was the highly regarded Multiple Management system, which I'd read and heard so much about, in action. What a break! I was about to have the advantage of witnessing Board veterans in action to serve as an example of how I should behave and present my upcoming project a little later. This was a stroke of real luck, I thought. Man, was I wrong.

The first guy up was a young Zone Manager from Pittsburgh named Dave Kuhns. I'd never heard of him. He began by talking something about the need for a sifter cap for our large Chef Size bottle of parsley flakes. Earth-shattering, I thought. How much research did he put into this one?

Suddenly, he stopped with the formal stuff, looked around the room at us, and said, "Ya know, I can make my point better by dramatizing what goes on today in thousands of kitchens across our great country." (Today, I know now that Dave can never tell a story without acting it out personally.)

With that, as God is my witness, he reached under the conference table, brought out a large kitchen pot and spoon, and slammed them on the conference table in front of him. From the pot he pulled out a very feminine, frilly apron, tied it around his waist, and began acting out the perfect example of the stereotypical "little woman" preparing dinner for her working husband that evening. His whistling and high-pitched feminine voice were terrific. Then he made a sound like a doorbell . . . "Ding-dongggg." This was quickly followed with, "Oh hello, Honey-Sweetie-Poopsie. Home so soon? Dinner will be ready shortly, Honey-Sweetie-Poopsie. Just relax for a minute, my Sweetie . . . " He really laid it on thick and I was asking myself, "Who in the hell is this guy?"

Well, just then, as he continued stirring his (her) imaginary spaghetti in this huge pot, he reached over and grabbed the spice. As he did so, still in this extremely feminine voice, he said, "Oh boy! Time for the McCormick parsley flakes." With that he unscrewed the cap from our largest Chef Size bottle, raised it over the pot, and with one shake the contents of the entire bottle emptied all over the kettle, table, tablecloth, and general area in front of him. Everything you could see was covered with parsley flakes. With that somber Kuhns look, he gazed seriously into the imaginary living room where his honey-sweetie-poopsie husband was relaxing, and screamed, "Ah #!!@!! Honey! Look what McCormick has done to my spaghetti dinner! It's ruined!!!"

The place roared its approval, and the Board unanimously passed his project for a new shaker top. How could you turn that down?

As we write this book, "sifter cap" Dave Kuhns has been promoted to McCormick/Schilling Vice President, Sales-East.

Dave Kuhns tells a couple of his own, this one having to do with the Paul Irwin "death march." Paul was sent down to the Light Street building to become the new General Manager of the Grocery Products Division (later renamed McCormick/Schilling Division). This was at the time of the introduction of our new "Project 1" packaging, which replaced most of the old "tin cans" and various bottles with new clear plastic bottles and entirely new graphics. "P1" was to be a great success but not without much investment, both in capital and marketing dollars. Initial

PEPPER PEOPLE

sales actually declined as the new line was introduced. The con-
figuration of the package reduced the number of packages on the
shelf, which created a one-time inventory reduction. The one
dozen pack on many items was reduced to one-half dozen, which
further reduced inventory. Good for the grocer, but temporarily
tough for McCormick sales. The new package design confused
some consumers for awhile, particularly in ethnic neighborhoods.
Therefore, the combination of the high expense of introducing the
new line and lower than expected sales contributed to a less than
satisfactory return to the Division in 1987.

Enter Paul Irwin. Paul was brilliant in turning the Division
around during his tenure as General Manager. One of his high
priorities was expense control, which earned the former marketer
a new Company-wide reputation as a real "hands-on" manager.

Paul always set the tone for expense control through example.
Dave relates this tale, which he calls the "Paul Irwin first annual
luggage pull." It happened at the Food Marketing Institute (FMI)
Convention, May 7, 1989:

> We arrived in Chicago and were gathering our luggage,
> when Paul suggested we all take the train into downtown
> Chicago. He said it was a wonderful ride, and it only cost
> $1.00.
> Normally, we would take the bus, which is $16.00 round
> trip. However, it did sound nice . . . a train ride into Chicago.
> Of course, the fact that the General Manager suggested it had
> no impact on our decision.
> There we were, loaded down with business clothes for
> four days of convention, plus evenings; and since we're all ath-
> letes, we also had our exercise gear. Plus, we had briefcases
> and boxes of brochures, account files, etc. for many customers
> and McCormick side meetings. I had a stuffed suit bag, a 400-
> pound suitcase, and a 100-pound briefcase.
> The first adventure occurred as we departed the luggage
> carousels. The airport train station was a good half-mile away,
> through corridors, down stairs, around corners, and finally to
> the ticket booth, through a turnstile, and down an escalator.
> Still more hiking to the train platform.
> We already knew we had made a bad, bad decision, but

here came the train! We boarded our luggage, which for the five of us took up practically one entire car.

Now . . . there is a feeling of adventure and romance when you think about a train; however, that's reserved for the trains that travel the mountains, rivers, and plains. Our train stopped a dozen times, and the scenery consisted of graffiti-covered buildings and other buildings ready to be razed. We also saw some interesting activities on the porches and backyards by the occupants, which I won't describe.

We finally reached downtown, and Paul decided the next stop was ours. We gathered our luggage and waited to exit the train, not knowing Paul was three stops off, and then the real acid test began.

As we departed the platform, we had to pass through another turnstile. This one was enclosed in a very narrow cage, which would not accept anything larger than a briefcase. We struggled with that for a while until we realized the only solution was to hoist each piece over the cage, which was at least ten feet high. This required much teamwork and certainly helped to bring us closer together. At this point, we still hadn't realized we had gotten off three stops too early.

Just beyond turnstile security we came face to face with the next challenge. Train stations are generally below street level in downtown areas, and this was no exception. We faced what appeared to be a skyscraper of stairs. We had to scale at least eight flights of steep concrete steps, this after hoisting and shoving our way around and through the turnstile. We were starting to wear out, and we still hadn't realized we were three stops too early.

We reached the street after what seemed forever, and I think we were all happy at this point, primarily because no one had yet experienced cardiac problems. It was then we met the "straw that broke the camel's back." As we searched the horizon for our Hyatt Hotel, we realized we were sixteen blocks away. You can imagine how good the cabs started looking. Mutiny was in the air.

However, we all silently agreed not to be embarrassed by the General Manager, so we began the "death march" segment of the trip. Block after block ensued, and all the happy chatter

died by the time we finally dragged into the hotel, hot, tired, sweaty, and wrinkled.

And you guessed it: "Your rooms won't be ready for five hours!"

Later that evening over cocktails, we relived the trip, and actually felt better for the experience. We also decided this was such a great experience that others should be able to participate. We created an annual competitive event, which would pit each contestant against the clock, and named it the "Paul Irwin Annual Luggage Pull."

Unfortunately, by the time FMI 1990 rolled around, we lost our enthusiasm, and the "Second Annual Luggage Pull" was not pulled off!

Dave Kuhns is a big guy, and he had trouble staying in his office chair. A number of times, while he was leaning back, it rolled out from under him and caused quite a commotion. One day he walked into his office and found a seat belt strapped to his chair, a hard hat on the chair, and the following letter on his desk top:

Office of The Secretary
Occupational Health and Safety Administration
(OSHA)

January 11, 1990

Mr. David E. Kuhns
McCormick & Co., Inc.
211 Schilling Circle
Hunt Valley, MD 21031

Dear Mr. Kuhns,

It has come to our attention that you have had an excessive number of incidental and consequential occurrences while on the job. Your Workmen's Compensation representative advises that you have failed to report any of the aforementioned lapses into clumsily oafish behavior.

This is the first report of such blatant unbalance ever recorded in Maryland. Incidents of a similar nature invariably occur in Western Pennsylvania when those Mill Hunkies try to squeeze their fat asses into swivel chairs. I'm sure there must be another explanation for your particular problem . . . . You're *not* a Mill Hunky, are you?? Please advise via return mail as to the dimensions of your posterior.

The request for this investigation comes from a female on the second floor, east wing of the McCormick/Schilling Center. She insists that on a regular basis, the *buffoon* (her words, not mine) above her office usually is unseated by a contrary office chair. The impact is enough to cause her considerable stress, but the unbridled profanity that follows is without parallel, except in one particular truck stop just outside of Greensburg, PA.

Mr. Kuhns, if this were an isolated incident, you may rest assured the agency would not get involved. We would consider dropping our investigation if we were to receive a sworn and notarized agreement that you will do the following:

1. Have your sense of balance tested by a certified specialist.
2. Wear a seat belt at all times.
3. Put your hard hat on before reaching for your phone.
4. Do not use a plastic chair mat.
5. Use your computer on your desk, not on your credenza.
6. Never use anything as dangerous as a speaker phone.
7. Wear arch supports and an athletic supporter at all times when on the job.

8. Sound a 10 second warning at 106.4 decibels when you plan to do it again.
9. Be certain to have a minimum of 3 witnesses.
10. Try to redistribute your weight.
11. Apologize to all within ear shot for the inappropriate, although colorful, language.
12. Check into Johns Hopkins to be evaluated for possible reversal of your lobotomy.

Mr. Kuhns, we would certainly welcome an amiable settlement of this issue. Don't make us get nasty. Jimmy Hoffa was the last guy we sent this letter to.

Best regards,
"BIG BROTHER"

And from former Sales Board member Marlin Sanderson, we derive more insight into that prominent body of executives:

In 1972, Chuck Graham was elected to succeed me as Chairman of the McCormick Division Sales Board. Chuck selected Walter Brown to be his Secretary.

At the conclusion of each Sales Board, one of the first duties of the new Chairman was to preside over a meeting with the Executive Committee of the Sales Board and top management, to present all of the recommendations that had been approved by the Sales Board. This presentation was made to the Director of Sales and usually two or three other management people whom the Director had invited to sit in.

Before these meetings, the Executive Committee of the Sales Board would spend several tense hours preparing for this presentation, organizing materials, samples, etc., and of course mapping the strategy we would use to try and sell our recommendation to management so it would be implemented. This was a very stressful time for all of us on the Executive Committee, particularly the new Chairman, who would actually make all the presentations. Members of the Sales Board and their contributions were on the line. If management was pleased with most of the recommendations, then the Sales Board had had a successful session. If we had very few or none that eventually got implemented, then the Sales Board had not performed well, in our opinion, so emotions ran high at these meetings.

To break up the tensions and have a little fun, Chuck Graham and I cooked up this trick to play on Walter Brown, the newly elected Secretary of the Sales Board (second in command).

After the Executive Committee had completed all its work and was well organized for the presentation, we had approximately two hours until our appointment with the Director of Sales. Chuck and I had rigged up a gin bottle filled with water and we had olives and lemon wedges on the bar. As I recall, the Executive Committee consisted of Chuck Graham, Walter Brown, Bud Roth, and me. We had all agreed to start dropping subtle hints to Walter Brown about how nervous we were, and what a pressured job it was to make this presentation to management, and how well prepared one must be to have everything go off smoothly. Also, we had dropped several casual remarks about the Secretary of the Board, being second in the chain of command, and if anything should happen to the Chairman, the Secretary would take over his duties.

With all of this groundwork laid, Chuck began acting very uptight and nervous, and told Walter he might have to ask him to make the presentation, because he was so nervous. This did not sit too well with Walter. He assured Chuck that his nervousness would pass, that the Executive Committee would be there to back him up, and he would be okay. Chuck continued to appear more nervous and suggested we all have a drink. Walter was the first to object to any drinks. He said in one hour we had our meeting. Chuck just had to have a martini and then decided that a double would be even better to calm him down. Chuck poured a water glass full from the "fixed" gin bottle with a couple of olives. Walter began to really get worried as Chuck tossed down the water glass full of gin. He proceeded to pour another drink of the same amount and consumed it in record time.

Now all of us were talking to Chuck and telling him to stop drinking, that he had already had too much, and he might not be able to make the presentation. By now, Chuck was really beginning to show the effects of his "drinks," talking loudly, slurring his words, and walking unsteadily. Walter Brown was beside himself at this point. He started running around telling everyone that Chuck was getting too drunk, and we had to sober him up. It was now approximately thirty minutes until presentation time, and Chuck was acting roaring drunk!

Walter went to the phone and ordered room service to send up two pots of coffee and tomato juice. He wanted us all to help him get Chuck in the shower to sober him up. By this time, it was only about ten minutes before our presentation, and Walter was going crazy, saying, "How could Chuck do this to us at such an important time?" He said, "What in the hell are we going to do? I'm not prepared properly to make this presentation. I was depending on Chuck. This is his job, not mine, and here he is roaring drunk and out of his mind. He's really messed us up today!"

With that statement, and because time had about run out, Chuck suddenly became sober as a judge, and we all started laughing. Walter could not believe his eyes. I have never seen a more relieved person in my life than Walter Brown, to see Chuck sober and ready to perform his duty. Walter was "off the hook."

All these antics cover up a great camaraderie and pride as was evidenced by J.P. Bergeron, Zone Manager from New Orleans. At a sales meeting, several field managers were asked to talk about their zones and customer base. Each manager described his zone, including which customers were sold as well as which were unsold. As J.P. approached the podium, he spoke into the microphone in a very loud and booming voice that emphasized his Cajun environment. "I am J.P. Bergeron from New Orleans, and we sell everybody!" And he did. Old Clarence Miller would have loved that.

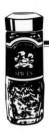

Chapter Nine

The Saga of The Hunt Valley Inn

McCormick Properties, originally called Maryland Properties, was formed to create the Hunt Valley Industrial Park.

In the late 1960s and early 1970s, a bare tract of land was transformed almost overnight into a bustling industrial beehive of activity. With the emergence of corporate offices and large business complexes, it became clear that there was a need for a facility capable of housing conventions and meetings, not to mention visiting guests and dignitaries of the business community. And to that end, The Hunt Valley Inn was born.

The Inn was a dramatically designed building, reminiscent of an old English castle. The 80-bedroom facility was first-class from the boiler room to the McCormick Suite, with every brick transported from England, and the finest in paintings, tapestries, flooring, and furnishings filling the lavish interior. Build the best . . . someone will stay in it!

Once completed, a staff was required to operate this well-oiled and exceptional facility. Once again, only the best would do, and a staff was built from some of the finest names in the hotel business. McCormick was well pleased with the Inn, and rightly so. It was a magnificent structure, beautifully appointed, and professionally staffed. The guests of the Inn entered the premises and were at once treated with the excellence synonymous with the name McCormick, while at the same time feeling as though they had come "home" to the comfort and friendliness so often longed for by the weary traveler.

As time passed, it became clear that the one thing desperately needed and heretofore missing at the Inn was someone connected

*In 1969, the Company moved to Hunt Valley and built
The Hunt Valley Inn.*

to McCormick – someone who would not only continue the tradition of excellent service to the public, but would assure McCormick that the runaway red ink might, in fact, turn black.

Several young men were chosen for the task, and on a bright day in 1973, the doors burst open and Dorsey Baldwin and Bill Adams were thrust upon an unsuspecting hotel staff. With virtually no hotel experience whatsoever, other than having been guests of other facilities themselves, Dorsey and Bill blew into that facility like a breath of fresh air, or a hot blast from Satan's furnace, depending on who was telling the tale. Like a dynamic duo somewhere between the Lone Ranger and Elliott Ness, they grabbed the reins of that runaway expenditure and made a little history. Despite his lack of experience in the business, Dorsey decided that selling was the same regardless of the product and turned his talents toward room sales, the convention and banquet business. Bill hit the ground running and didn't stop until he had landed in the Accounts Receivable department, where panic was the word of the day. Let the games begin!!

One of the first pieces of business for Bill was putting a lid on the amount of theft occurring in-house. It's an occupational hazard in the hotel/restaurant business, and a minimal amount of pilferage is usually accepted. But everything that wasn't tied down grew legs and walked right out of the many exits. Security was a nightmare. Fire laws prevented the exit doors from being locked on the inside, and having a guard posted at every exit would have been prohibitive. Bill, now having been put in charge of security, devised a system whereby all Hunt Valley Inn employees had to leave from one exit. Any bags, boxes, carryalls, etc. were subject to inspection by the one guard posted at the exit. There were several guards hired for the position, since the hotel business is a 24-hour-a-day enterprise, and staff members worked in shifts.

Several days into the new security plan, Bill arrived at the Inn one morning and decided to check with the "exit" guard. Just as Bill reached the checkpoint, he saw the guard stop an employee entering the building. With great precision and thoroughness, the employee's large shopping bag was meticulously checked before the guard allowed entry. Curious, Bill approached the guard and asked what he was doing. "Just checking the bag, Mr. Adams," he was told. Bill was incredulous, but patient. With calm deliberation he explained, "I don't care what the employees bring *inside*. I want to know what they take out!"

And take out they did. One of the focal points of the hotel lobby was a pair of exquisite Persian carpets, purchased at great expense and used mainly as welcome mats. It was doubtful whether the thousands of weary travelers who shuffled their dusty shoes across those carpets even noticed them. But someone did. Someone with excellent taste and a thirst for an adventurous gamble.

It was early Christmas Day . . . very early. Bill had by now discovered what every hotel man ultimately learns – you take the job home with you. With his family happily plowing through Christmas packages and wrapping paper, Bill slipped off to call the front desk to check on things. He spoke to the young lady on duty that morning, exchanged pleasantries and holiday greetings, and asked about the state of the Inn. Everything was just fine – very quiet, virtually empty, in fact. Almost as a postscript, the desk clerk added brightly, "Oh, by the way, Mr. Adams, the rug cleaners came." Bill spoke calmly but clearly: "What rug cleaners?"

"They came about an hour ago to take the Persians and have them cleaned."

"On Christmas Day?" Bill asked.

"Yeah, that's what I said," he was told, "but they said that was the best time to do that kind of stuff . . . when the place is empty. That way the guests aren't inconvenienced." Uh-huh.

The next call Bill made was to General Manager Irv Anderson. "Merry Christmas, Irv. Meet me at the Inn . . . I think we've been taken to the cleaners!"

That wasn't the only big-ticket item to take a hike. Two burly, overall-clad men waltzed into the foyer one bright day and in plain sight of dozens of guests and employees,

THE HUNT VALLEY INN

rolled a grand piano right out the door and into a moving van. No one said a word, not even "goodbye."

Ditto TV sets, velvet curtains, and spreads, as well as several lamps. Our Inn gave a whole new meaning to "curb service."

Often one of the most difficult tasks in the hotel business is keeping a well-trained staff on hand. It's a 24-hour-a-day, 365-day-a-year operation. The welcome mat must always be out. The reservations clerk constantly walked a thin line between overbooking and leaving rooms empty. Bill's favorite saying was, "Rent every room today – you can't rent them twice tomorrow." As with the airlines, you quickly learn when running a hotel that "no-shows" are going to happen. You gamble a little and hope for the best.

The one exception in those days was Preakness Weekend. Every room in Baltimore and the outlying areas was sold out. The Hunt Valley Inn was, too. Dorsey had worked his magic on Chick Lang (of Pimlico Race Course) and made arrangements for the selected dignitaries, owners, public figures, and jockeys involved with the running of the great race to stay at the Inn. The word went out to one and all: "All rooms are reserved and guaranteed – don't sell them."

Now, one of the worst things that can happen to a guest who has a reservation, especially an *important* guest, is to get "walked." That's hotel lingo for "shuffled off to Buffalo," or any nearby hotel that can take your overflow when you overbook and, quite frankly, screw up. Bill had been told by Dorsey that nothing must go wrong, least of all walking anyone. Bill, in turn, told his front desk staff . . . and told them . . . and told them again. All was in readiness for the big weekend.

On the morning of the Preakness race, very early, Bill called the Inn to check with his staff. Everything was fine. The house was full, and there were no problems – except for the late arrivals who got walked at 2:00 in the morning.

"Who got walked?" Bill asked.

"Some short guy . . . well, actually there were two of

them. They said they had a reservation, but when no one showed up by 1:00 A.M., I let the room go."

Bill could feel the sweat trickling down his back as a hideous premonition gripped him by the throat. "Who got walked?" he repeated.

There was a pause, then the worst possible words he could have heard zoomed through the phone wires. "Angel Cordero."

"You *walked* Angel Cordero?!" Bill screeched into the phone. "He just won the Kentucky Derby! He's the odds-on favorite to win today! And you WALKED him! We're dead. *I'm* dead. Dorsey will see to it!"

For a dead man, Bill was making an awful lot of noise as he thundered around the house, incredulous that his specific instructions to his staff had been so completely ignored. And the most outrageous thing was, the clerk actually had the audacity to add, "At least we rented the room."

Well, the wires burned that day. It turned out that Angel Cordero and another jockey had spent the night sleeping atop a banquet table at a nearby hotel. No sooner had the sun peeped over the window sill than Mr. Cordero was on the phone threatening to sue the Inn if he lost the Preakness race. Talk about a lot riding on a race – this was it.

If you're a racing fan, you'll remember that, in fact, Angel Cordero did *not* win that race. The only thing higher than Bill's blood pressure that day was the Goodyear blimp. The saving grace for the Inn was the fact that the jockey who was with Angel and spent the night on the accompanying banquet table *did* win. And he won riding the stable-mate to Angel's mount, with the same owner. Case closed. Not even Judge Wapner would have wanted that one.

If it seems like the front desk operation was of major importance, perhaps that's because it was. These were the days just preceding the computer age, when reservations were taken by phone and copied on small cards – cards that sometimes managed to get lost or misplaced or duplicated.

If, like most people, you have been on the receiving

end of a computer snafu and think nothing can be worse, think again! Don't sell human error short. It can be quite as complex and devastating as anything a machine can do – and then some.

In a perfect world, no one ever gets sick, or quits his job, or just fails to show up for work. Not so at the Inn. The worst moments were the times the night crew didn't show. The day shift would usually stay for a few minutes extra, but if it looked like an employee "no-show" they were out the door in a heartbeat. That's usually when Bill either enlisted the help of someone else on duty or stayed behind the desk himself . . . or asked his wife to report to work.

On one particularly hectic night, the switchboard operator failed to show up for work. (Remember, this was pre-computer age. The switchboard looked like something you would have seen in an old "I Love Lucy" episode – with lights and wires in tangled profusion, and definitely not the place for a novice.) Bill enlisted the help of a bellman who, to put it as politely as possible, had limited experience on a switchboard and even more limited capabilities for grasping the switchboard concept on the best day of his life. Even with everything cooking on all four burners, it was an error waiting to happen. But you do what you must, and Bill was already filling in for someone else who was gone.

(It's amazing how quickly you find out what the ultimate "no-no's" are in the hotel business. You never give out anyone's room number or a key to a room without proper identification, to name two. On two separate occasions, someone managed to commit these faux pas with disastrous consequences.)

With our young rocket scientist filling in at the switchboard, it was just a matter of time. Sure enough, it happened. One of the male guests at the Inn had just completed a call to his "sweetie" and was on the phone whispering in graphic detail (we later learned) just exactly what he intended to do with and/or to said lady later in the evening. Meanwhile, back at the desk, "Slick" was receiving a call from the man's frantic wife. Their son had broken his leg, and she was desperate to reach her husband. No problem. With the accuracy and precision of a brain surgeon, the young man spliced the two lines, making it possible for the distraught woman to now be privy to the rather libertine conversation between her husband and his "honey-pooh." The only thing that traveled through the Inn faster than the story itself were the divorce papers served to the guest with his breakfast tray.

On another occasion, the Inn was host to a very posh wedding and reception, followed by a very loud and disorderly gathering of the wedding party. When the reception had ended, a few diehards moved into the bar and continued to toast the happy couple, and anything else that moved. Late in the evening, a handsome, smiling young man approached the front desk and sheepishly asked for a key to the bridal suite.

"I'm sorry, sir," he was told. "We can't give out a key without identification."

"But, you don't understand," the young man explained. "I'm the groom. I had to go to the car for something and I've left my wallet and the room key back in the suite."

"I'm very sorry, but we cannot give out a key," the clerk stated.

The young man was very convincing. He was in a tuxedo, he knew the names of the room assigned, the address, the phone number, and insisted that his bride was in the bathtub and couldn't let him inside. He begged, he cajoled, he pleaded, he looked pitiful . . . and finally, he got the key, which he used to go to the bridal suite and catch the newlyweds in flagrante delicto! And, as if that weren't enough, he managed to take pictures!

What's a hotel without a fine restaurant? The Hunt Valley Inn boasted one of the best. A California artist was commissioned to design a life-sized tree of shimmering metal and copper: a Cinnamon Tree. It was constructed on the West Coast, then carefully taken apart, transported, and re-assembled in the center of the restaurant that would bear its name. A focal point of fine dining, it was a unique symbol of the quality and perfection that has made McCormick the success it is.

The Cinnamon Tree Restaurant became synonymous with excellence, from the tips of the intricately folded napkins to the twenty-two carat gold edging on the china plates. The clientele was top drawer, and they were to be offered nothing less when they dined. Neither, it seemed, would those who served it.

Several years ago, someone wrote a song about a factory worker in an automobile plant who took a piece of a car home in his lunch pail every day until, finally, he was able to assemble his own car. Surely, that must have been the reigning theme at the Cinnamon Tree as the china, silver, and table linens sprouted wings and flew away at a startling rate. Replacements were ordered on a daily basis. On one particular occasion, the General Manager gathered everyone together to discuss the possibility of ordering all new tableware with completely different designs and motif. "Absolutely not!" was Bill's vote. "The entire staff now has a complete service for twelve. The last thing we need to do is give them a new selection." They kept the original pattern.

The Cinnamon Tree offered not only the finest in ambience and excellent cuisine, but the most professional international staff as well. The waiters were Greek, Italian, French, and Swiss, and most of them spoke only enough English to handle orders from the menu and inquiries about the restrooms. But the one thing that would bring them together like a small United Nations convoy was a birthday. With wide grins and more gusto than talent, all of the waiters would gather around the celebrant, singing what sounded to the untrained ear like "Hoppity Birtray."

Though it might have sounded a bit rough around the edges, the amount of training that went into the teaching of that popular ditty was nothing short of that of an Olympic hopeful. But even more challenging than the birthday song, was the assignment Bill was given (short straw) to demonstrate to the Greek waiters how to use and apply deodorant. It was an experience that defies anything that can be put on paper.

Adjacent to the Cinnamon Tree were the banquet rooms, which thanks to Dorsey and his capable staff, were filled regularly with prestigious and influential guests. Will we ever forget Dorsey's "first" banquet? Everything had to be perfect. His reputation and that of the Inn rested on the success of that premiere and stellar occasion. The menu was incomparable, and the meal would be topped off with nothing less than cherries jubilee for dessert. At just the precise moment, the lights dimmed, strategically placed waiters struck matches, and the fun began. First the cherries caught fire . . . then the flambé table caught fire . . . then the drapes caught fire . . . are we having fun yet? Everyone was evacuated quickly, and nothing was hurt but Dorsey's pride and the first banquet waiter he reached after the fact.

Dorsey knew everyone. York Road was his backyard, and he never saw a stranger. He was always "on" and drumming up business . . . and nobody did it better. In an effort to increase the "regular" clientele, something new was added. The wine cellar, located between the Cinnamon Tree and the bar, seemed an ideal location for a nightspot, so "Gatsby's" was born – a cross between a bistro and a cabaret, and "the" place to be on a Thursday night.

At this time, there was a disc jockey on a Baltimore station who, for lack of a better description, can only be called the most radical and irreverent personage to ever hit the air waves. He made risqué seem like Sunday school and without doubt, he was the man most likely to say or do anything. He was, in short, just what Gatsby's needed.

Dorsey approached Irv and proposed that they hire Johnny Walker to host the events at Gatsby's on Thursday nights. Dorsey predicted that the liquor sales alone would make the investment worth it. The bar was bringing in about $700 a night, and Dorsey claimed they would see $2,700 from Gatsby's with the deejay on board. Irv was skeptical – so much so, in fact, that he promised to kiss Dorsey's posterior at the staff meeting if they pulled in that much money.

Johnny Walker showed up and began the night with a free gift giveaway to the first girl who reached him on the stage without her shirt on! The crowd went wild. They loved Johnny and his irreverent behavior. Gatsby's was on the map. And the first night's receipts were over $3,000.

Dorsey arrived at the staff meeting the next day, wearing only a bathrobe and a smile . . . and was completely ignored by Irv, who conducted the shortest staff meeting on record, then left without a word or glance at Dorsey.

Gatsby's became so popular that it was not unusual to see people lined up along the spiral staircase, unable to even get as far as the floor of the room. Every week was more outrageous than the last, and still the crowds came – and with them, profits.

Hilly (Hillsman) Wilson was the McCormick corporate officer responsible for the Inn. For the most part, Hilly said little as long as everything was in order and running well. However, with the news of Gatsby's spreading in ever-widening circles, he decided to check it out personally. With Dorsey in tow, Hilly approached the miniature night-club with its usual cadre of rabble, immediately noting that there were far too many people in so small a place. Lawyer Hilly assailed Dorsey with dire predictions about losing their license, etc. because of the fire marshal's regulations. Nothing Dorsey could say would ease Hilly's mind. So, Dorsey did the only thing he could think of to help the situation. He pulled Hilly down the stairs into the teeming throng of Gatsby regulars, right up to a man who was obviously having the time of his life, and none the worse for the drinks he had consumed. Then, flashing that famous Baldwin smile, Dorsey introduced Hilly to the fire marshal himself. Oh, yes, those were good old days!

One of the things absolutely verboten at the Inn was the presence of anyone "soliciting" on the premises. For the most part, this was easily enforced . . . with the exception of Ruthie. Try as they would, it was all but impossible to keep Ruthie out of the lobby and bar. Ruthie was, after all, a "working" girl, there with the blessing of her husband, who thoughtfully dropped her off every night. Bill confronted the night crew, the bellmen, Ruthie herself. He even made threats, sent memos, and tore large tufts of hair out of his head, to no avail. Ruthie stuck like glue and regardless of what was said or done, it was business as usual for her.

Bill stayed at the Inn late one night and as he was leaving, he stopped by the front desk. There, behind the counter, playing quietly on the floor, were two small children. It was late and Bill asked the obvious question, "Whose kids are those?"

The night clerk never even paused as he calmly stated, "Ruthie's . . . her husband was sick tonight and couldn't watch them." Et tu, Brutus? It's tough fighting City Hall.

We've already cited several hotel "no-no's," but perhaps the biggest one of all is a death in the house. It just doesn't happen. Oh, no – not *in* the house. Regardless of how "dead" a person was, he was *always* DOA at the hospital. A deceased hotel guest is anathema to the house and must be avoided at all costs. There was never any doubt when Housekeeping found a body. If the screaming got by you, there was no way you could miss the wide eyes, the flailing arms, and the look of horror in the eyes of the discoverer. Bill knew it was going to be a bad day when he could hear a scream on the third floor clear down in the ground floor office.

On one particular occasion, it looked like there would be no way to escape the dreaded publicity of an expired guest. The man had apparently departed this life early in the evening, and by the time he was discovered, rigor mortis had already set in; but hey – we'll give it a try.

Bill called the ambulance service and told them a guest had just had a heart attack. Moments later, the crew arrived and was led to the victim. One glance at the man was all that was needed to send eyebrows clear into the hairlines of those three men. "*Just* had a heart attack? Yeah, right!"

By now, Dorsey had arrived, and he and Bill had to figure out a way to get the dead man resurrected and declared DOA at the hospital. The crew was busy loading the man onto a stretcher, and time was running out. Then, Dorsey pulled one of the men aside. "How does this sound? All expenses paid, best rooms in the house, free food and booze, weekend of your choice for you guys and your wives . . . . What do you say?" The men talked it over for a few minutes, then returned and declared that perhaps they had been a bit hasty. Maybe there was a slight pulse-beat after all. Anyone watching must have wondered about the poor man on the stretcher, covered with a sheet, his right arm sticking straight out, stiff as a board.

Memories of the days at the Inn bring smiles, sometimes outright laughter, as we recall the lighter moments. Bill's wife was often enlisted to fill in for people out sick or on vacation. She could be found doing just about everything but K.P. and housekeeping. Drew worked the reservation desk, where outrageous things happened on a regular basis. Sonny James once called for a room at a time when the Inn was completely booked – actually, overbooked. In an effort to get a room he *sang* to her, but you can't give away what you don't have, so Sonny James had to go elsewhere.

Drew once spotted the Orkin man just as he got on the elevator on his way up to the lobby, his exterminating equipment in hand. Only by removing her high heels and running full speed, shoeless, up the stairs was she able to stop him from parading right through the busiest section of the Inn. As the Bicentennial year approached, she greeted a man there to make plans for a celebration banquet and actually managed to keep a straight face every time he said "bicententacle."

But of her Hunt Valley Inn memories, the very best was New Year's Eve 1974. The Inn was sold out, and it was partytime! Bill was the Manager on Duty that night, and Drew was working the switchboard. As the evening progressed, the crowd got more raucous, and it was without a doubt a case of the inmates running the asylum. The safest place to be was behind the desk.

For most of the evening, things were quiet . . . until midnight. At the stroke of twelve, that monster board with its gazillion lights and wires lit up like an airport runway. Everyone in the Free World was trying to call someone at The Hunt Valley Inn. No one could have handled that particular task, least of all someone who had only done the job a half-dozen times before. When the call came in from London, England, Drew saw her chance to abandon the board. A very inebriated, veddy British gentleman asked if she would sing "Melancholy Baby" for him. It must have seemed strange to others, having the switchboard operator singing in the midst of all that confusion, but it sure beat trying to answer all those other calls!

Those stories were related to us by none other than our singing operator, Drew Adams. Husband Bill, along with Dorsey Baldwin, eventually moved on to the McCormick/Schilling Division, where they became partners again, pinching more pennies and wooing more new customers.

If the competition reads this chapter, one would hope that they might be inclined to throw in the towel.

Here's some more, this time from Bill Adams:

Dorsey Baldwin and I had difficult assignments at The Hunt Valley Inn. The Hunt Valley Inn had developed a very bad reputation as a negative cash flow for the Corporation. Dorsey's assignment was to build volume and change the image, and my assignment was to make it cash sufficient.

Dorsey had been entertaining various customers in an effort to get them to be familiar with and appreciate the facilities and services the Inn had to offer. It just so happens that his entertainment expense was extremely high and somewhat impacted our cash flow. I met with Dorsey, discussed the matter with him, and told him that in good conscience I could not support those kinds of entertainment expenses. Well, Dorsey set me up. He told me that if I thought entertaining customers was all easy, and guaranteed me that if I would go with him for the next five nights in a row entertaining customers, he would personally pay for the expense report that I thought was inappropriate.

We started on Monday night. Dorsey came down to my office around 7:00 P.M. and picked me up. I took enough cash to last the week. We met the customers and started off with dinner, drinks, a tour of the facility, a tour of the area, a tour of Baltimore, etc. To make a long story short, sometime about two hours before bars closed, we ran out of money. With that, Dorsey prevailed upon Al Walsh, Food and Beverage Manager, to sing in the bar, and made an announcement to the crowd that if they would buy us drinks, Al Walsh would sing any request. Al did have a beautiful voice. He received about five different requests. Al sang "Danny Boy" to each one.

The crowd continued to buy us drinks until the bar closed. Each night thereafter, up through Thursday night, it got worse. The customers, of course, loved it. They booked business, and I was about to die. On Friday evening, Dorsey came to pick me up for my fifth and final experience. I was shaking; my mind and eyes no longer functioned. I told Dorsey that I would never again challenge his expense reports, if he would agree to never take me with him again.

The marriage between McCormick people and those in the hotel business was difficult in its early stages. With Dorsey and me representing McCormick, we usually bore the brunt of criticism for those months that we could not make financial objectives. In the early days, this was frequent. Dorsey and I dreaded the meetings because they were more or less a rat court for us.

Our General Manager had somehow indicated to us that he thought the back lot was being used for purposes other than just parking cars. He indicated an interest in seeing it for himself. Dorsey and I made up a beautiful blonde in a white Mustang. At the time we knew the meetings were going to be less than pleasant, we would agree to bring up the fact that the white Mustang was on the back lot. When that occurred, the meeting was usually canceled immediately, and the General Manager and Chief of Security would storm the hill on all fours, military style, in an effort to observe the car. They, of course, were always too late. With this example of 2 for 1 spirit, Dorsey and I were able to delay our monthly reviews until such time as they were pleasant.

And then came the evening of a Multiple Management Board dinner – a Henry VIII banquet. In "Old McCormick" style, it turned into a shambles. Jack Thompson survived to tell us about it:

There was every kind of food flying. The violinist, who was the noted Baltimore bandleader, Zim Zemarel, was in the kitchen holding a towel full of ice against his eye, which was swollen. Hit with a grape.

Somebody threw a corn cob and knocked over the candelabra, which spilled some hot wax, burning our home economist, Toni Manning.

Earlier in the evening, the banquet manager had asked me to get the party moving a little bit. Was he kidding? Get it moving! Later on he came and demanded that we cease our operations, but by then it was too late. We were all too far gone.

The finale was peach shortcake. Everybody proceeded to smash everybody else in the face, in the back, wherever they could, with the dessert.

At one point, I remember Jim Harrison grabbing for Evelyn DeGast of Corporate Communications, slipping on the shortcake, and rolling under the table.

This was also the night that Hilly Wilson, Don Dick, and Jim Harrison were coming back from Easthampton, Massachusetts following discussions on the new Tubed Products facility financing. That's the same night that Don Dick, our Treasurer, was apprehended by the FBI for referring to bombs in connection with airplanes at the boarding gate.

The next day Ed Vinnecombe, Vice President of Corporate Communications, was very proud. He said the spirit of McCormick was still riding high, but he didn't think it was so funny when he got a bill for $3,000 to fix up the Garden Room, including the wine stains on the pictures on the wall.

Every once in a while when I get together with some of the old guys, we recall this as one of the highlights of our MM Board experiences.

Another of the young pepper people sent over to the Inn was Carroll Nordhoff. Carroll handled Human Relations, and later, Sales and Marketing. He recounted these beauties:

A senior executive from another company was transferred to the Baltimore area to oversee the opening of a major new facility of his company. He was staying in Baltimore for some months and made his home at The Hunt Valley Inn. He would travel on weekends, but Sunday night through Thursday night he was our resident guest.

Unfortunately, one night in the wee hours, the gentleman experienced some health distress that subsequently led to a heart attack and his death. This is sad in itself, but the sadder part came when the maid found him in his bathroom the next morning. He apparently slept without clothes on. Feeling discomfort during the night, he went to the bathroom, where he had his heart attack and died. The bathroom door was slightly closed. The maid, entering the next morning, did not discover his body right away, but proceeded to clean the guest room. She had to force the bathroom door open (remember, his body was lodged behind it.) Upon seeing the dead, nude male, she went screaming not only out of the room, but out of the hotel, headed north on foot at about twenty miles per hour. The last words we ever heard her speak, as she ran through our lobby with her hands waving madly in the air, were, *"He's dead!!! He's dead!!!"* All attempts to find her for the purpose of final paychecks proved fruitless. As far as we know, she's still headed north.

One of our best bar customers of all time, a local executive from a prominent company, appeared naked in the lobby at about 3:00 A.M., obviously having had a few (too many?) drinks plus a moonlight swim in the pool. Whether Willie swam by himself or not was a question we did not ask. The night auditor, quick on his feet, sprang to action and commandeered a robe from our Housekeeping Department so that Willie would be clothed.

When asked where his clothes were, Willie really couldn't remember. When we got some black coffee into

Willie and asked him if we could arrange transportation to his home, he responded that everything was fine. He had called his wife to come pick him up. When his wife arrived on the scene, it was obvious that she was not a happy camper. And Willie, having had just enough coffee to recognize the severity of the moment, immediately changed his story and claimed that he had been mugged and stripped, whereupon the police were called. Although the case never went any further, we lost a good customer that evening, because Willie was never seen again.

One of the cardinal rules in a hotel is that hotel employees never frequent a guest room, particularly when the guest room is occupied. Early in the days of the Inn, we had one female employee who was absolutely outstanding and was, because of her great disposition and talent, a true utility infielder, working enormous hours and doing a variety of jobs.

Unfortunately, our valuable employee was found exiting an occupied guest room at 7:00 A.M. Through investigation, we found that the room was occupied by a person who was well known to this young lady. He was an old childhood sweetheart who had moved out of town and was in town briefly for business. Given the gravity of the situation, we felt there was no recourse other than termination of employment. When her then current supervisor, a middle-aged male known to enjoy himself on occasion, sat down with the Human Relations Manager to notify her of her termination of employment, she responded, "You've got to be kidding. What could possibly be wrong with a roll in the hay with an old friend?" When neither the H.R. manager nor the supervisor could think of a good answer, it was agreed to call it a three-day suspension, and her employment status continued.

So much for our hotel days. We finally gave up, asked Marriott to take over the management of the hotel, and eventually sold the hotel to the Prudential Life Insurance Company.

We had come a long way. After all, the first McCormick dinner was ended in dramatic style. We were entertaining the financial executives, and after dinner in came one of the waitresses with a cigar box. She passed out the cigars at the first table, and nobody took one until she got to Chairman Harry Wells. When offered the cigars, Harry said, "Great . . . I think I'll have several" and picked three from the box. The waitress panicked, screamed, "You only get one," and tore the two extras right out of the surprised Chairman's hand. With that, and at breakneck speed, she toured the room and dealt *everyone* one cigar.

The second memorable dinner involved our partners from Mexico. We again used the Garden Room. It's difficult enough eating in foreign countries because often the cuisine is so different. But this night, neither the Mexicans nor the Americans could eat the entrée – some kind of glopped-up chicken piled high, surrounded with other stuff, and covered with goop. It was terrible! Of course, since we were so proud of our new Inn, and with the Mexicans as our guests, nobody mentioned the food. However, what got carried in, got carried out. The Mexicans, I have noticed, never eat in The Hunt Valley Inn to this day, forsaking it for Obrycki's Crab House.

The financial group tried again, this time with a banquet concluding a three-day meeting that included all the corporate officers and members of the Board of Directors, as well as division heads. It was customary at this banquet for the Corporate Controller to call on the newest member of the financial staff to make some remarks about his first experience at the financial conference. On this particular evening, the Corporate Controller called on the newest member of the financial staff of The Hunt Valley Inn to make a few remarks.

The newest member had had several drinks during the cocktail hour and had continued celebrating his first financial conference with wine through dinner and several drinks after dinner. Needless to say, it was a surprise to this individual to be called on. It was difficult to rise from his seat, much less say a few remarks. With a great deal of difficulty, two or three minutes of incoherent remarks were offered and the member mercifully sat down. However, within a few short moments, he was up again to finish what he thought was a substantive message to all the other members of the conference. It was during this second phase that the celebrating really caught up with this person. In a rush, he made for the exit but barely made it out of the dining room before losing his dinner on the Oriental rugs that had been placed in the hallway of the Inn. You'll be happy to know he survived this incident, succeeded in future endeavors, and became an important member of management in the Company.

Never let it be said that lessons aren't learned from traumatic experiences.

After the sale of the Inn, three McCormick employees benefited one evening from knowledge that had wafted out of McCormick's experiences in the lodging and hospitality business. The trio was visiting Club House Foods in London, Ontario, and had just come in from the airport and were waiting to be checked into the Holiday Inn. Gus Theobald and Mike Sharman took turns brow beating the room clerk and were told that there "were no rooms left." The twosome, well relaxed from their flight from Baltimore, started making a "big" scene, yelling and shouting at the poor room clerk.

Purchasing Head Stan Godwin, a soft-spoken North Carolinian, tapped Gus on the shoulder. Stan, a vice president of McCormick, was the senior individual. Stan said, "Guys, please don't act that way. It doesn't reflect well on the Company. Please let me handle this."

So Stan went to the head of the line and said to the room clerk, "Excuse me, sir, is my understanding correct that you have our reservations, but that there are no rooms available to give us?" The room clerk now smiled for the first time in many minutes and said, "That's quite right, sir. I'm very sorry, but we seem to be oversold this evening." But he didn't know that Stan knew that every hotel holds back a few rooms even when oversold. Stan then said, this time very quietly, "I understand your problem."

He looked at his watch and said, "Under the circumstances, we'll just go on down to one of the restaurants and have some dinner. We'll be back at 9:30 . . . and if we don't have three single rooms waiting for us, I'll knock your #!!@!! teeth right down your throat." With that he turned and again quietly joined his two companions. "Now that's how you handle a situation like this." Three rooms were ready when they returned at 9:30.

Chapter Ten

Some All-Time McCormick Characters

H. ROBERT SHARMAN

I was hoping to get a stockman's job, but all they had open was a window washer's job. Looking at the building, I saw it was all windows. So, being a smart ass, I said that it looked like a steady job to me, so I'll take it.

The first day they put me in the stockroom, which I liked, and I worked part of the second day there. Then I was told that they needed a man in the spice mill, and I was sent up there. Bill Fowble was in charge then, so he took me in tow, gave me a large dusting brush, and told me to dust off each mill. I did pretty well until I hit the third mill, which was the red pepper mill. I started dusting and began to get real hot. I opened my collar and got hotter, rolled up my sleeves and was on fire. It got so bad that I went down to the desk and told Rex Welch that I had to quit dusting because I could hardly see. Rex said, "Well, Bob, if you can't do the job we will have to let you go." Rex called Bill Fowble, who came up and took me to the men's room, turned on the hot water, and told me to lather my hands real good and rub the lather well into my face. That was like putting a match to dynamite. It was so bad they literally hung me out the window on track-side to let the air cool me off.

I went home that night and told my wife Regina that there was no way I would ever go back to McCormick. She reminded me that jobs were scarce and that we needed the

198

money very badly. This was in 1936. So the next day I went back. As I was climbing the front steps Bill Fowble met me, put his arm around me, and said, "Son, you are the last person that I thought would come through that door today. With that determination you should have a job here for as long as you like." I lasted thirty-nine years.

Bob Sharman would be my choice as captain of the all-time McCormick characters. Bob was naturally funny, but he pushed the limit when it came to creating "shock value." No one has ever observed Bob having been punched out by strangers after some of his antics, but that's pretty amazing.

When I was working in the Human Relations Department, I received a call from a clothier uptown, recommending that we interview his secretary. He was letting her go because of lack of business. We agreed to the interview, and in came one of the prettiest young blonde ladies you have ever seen. She was also very shy and had only worked in a one-person office.

We hired her and sent her up to the general office on the eighth floor at our Light Street building. The general office was a large open area, and in the center of it all was Bob Sharman, who was then Credit Manager.

When the pretty young girl arrived, Sharman and some of the others went crazy and started pounding on the steel file cabinets. Every time she walked into the office, after lunch, and after tea breaks, the joyous beating on the files repeated. That was her first and last day of work. She never showed up again.

While he was Credit Manager, Sharman was in charge of writing "ding" letters to delinquent accounts. One such account was run by a loudmouth Brooklynite who was known to be armed. With Sharman scheduled to visit the area and make some calls on the trade, Al Ireland arranged the meeting. Sharman was briefed on what a soft-spoken, religious, and gentle person he was about to meet and was cautioned to behave himself.

So, when Sharman was introduced as Credit Manager, the customer jumped up from his desk, drew the gun from its holster, and shouted, "So you are the S.O.B. who writes those *%#@!# nasty 'ding' letters." The red-headed, bespectacled Sharman turned ghost white as he was chased out of the store and down the street.

Here's a Sharman story as told by Howard Dickerson, a sales and marketing executive in the McCormick/Schilling Division. Howard had just been transferred to Dallas:

> I was thirty-one years old, a brand new Zone Manager trying to make a good impression. The first day in the office went very well. We spent most of the day reviewing accounts, personnel, etc. That evening Bob said, "Since Alice is still in Baltimore, and you are temporarily in a hotel till she moves, why not have dinner with me tonight and we can continue our discussion."
>
> Needless to say I was excited. The first day went well and here is the Regional Sales Manager having dinner with me to further review the zone. Well, nothing could have been further from the truth.
>
> I was told to go to my hotel, freshen up, and meet Bob at the old Black Garter Club in the Executive Hotel by Love Field at 8:00 P.M. I went to my room and for the next two hours studied like crazy in anticipation of a lot of questions. We got to the Black Garter Club and ordered drinks. We were seated at a table next to the bandstand and dance floor. We had another drink and another, until all at once the band came out and started playing. The trumpet player and leader of the band looked just like Al Hirt. The place was packed. All at once, Bob Sharman started needling the band, especially the leader on trumpet. I thought he was a great trumpet player, but Bob continued his tirade with, "Who taught you to play trumpet? I've heard better music on a street corner."
>
> Needless to say, I was totally embarrassed and didn't know quite how to handle this situation. Here I was totally prepared to discuss business, and we were sitting on top of the band as Bob continued to badger the bandleader. More drinks came, and it got louder and louder. Finally, after so much, the spotlight came on us and I could have died. People were staring and laughing, and at the same time wondering who these two drunks were.
>
> Bob was a master. He and the bandleader went back

and forth for at least five minutes. I figured this was the end of my career. First day on the job in Dallas and here we are about to go to jail or end up in a fight. Next thing I knew, the bandleader called Bob up to the bandstand and said, "Ladies and gentlemen! Let's hear it for Bob Sharman, one of the greatest straight men of all time."

Then I realized it was all a set-up by Bob to introduce me to the Dallas nightlife. He brought the bandleader over to our table, introduced me, and we had a great time the rest of the evening. Never did discuss business. For one brief moment in time I knew I was history. Bob was the greatest, and there will never be another like him.

I had similar experiences with Sharman. While involved in test marketing the product "Fun" in southern Florida, Bob, who was Florida District Manager at that time, put me up in the Travelers Hotel across from the Miami Airport.

Bob knew everyone in the place, and the first night he told me to go into the lounge. He would come by and meet me after dinner. There was a very funny entertainer, who played the piano and told jokes on stage. About break time, the entertainer announced that he was going to take a break and have a little snack. With that he brought out a lady's "falsie" in one hand and with the other sprinkled it with a can of 4-ounce McCormick pepper. Obviously another set-up by Sharman.

While District Manager in Florida, Sharman was visited by his Regional Manager from Atlanta, Bill Naylor. They were supposed to meet in the morning, with Sharman providing the transportation. The only problem was that Sharman was out partying the night before down on Key Biscayne. At a late hour, he put his car in reverse by mistake and backed it over a sea wall, rendering the rear wheels useless. Sharman met Naylor at 8:00 A.M. all right, but in the form of being towed up to the front of the hotel by a tow truck!

Sharman loved to grab microphones. One day he slipped into the vestibule of an American Airlines DC-6 and made the departure announcement just as people were getting seated. He started off with, "You have just finished the most dangerous part of your trip, your drive to the airport." He kept talking as the stewardesses laughed, but the Captain finally came running back to see who the culprit was. When the four-striper pulled back the curtain and exposed Sharman, the red head screamed, thus ending the charade.

With a group down on the "Baltimore Block," Sharman led them upstairs to the old Piccadilly Club, the raunchiest of all local establishments. After a few minutes we all realized that the Master of Ceremonies was terribly untalented. Sharman took care of that by walking up on stage and taking the microphone away from him. The M.C. was so amazed he did nothing, and Sharman directed the show for the next hour.

After he became Regional Manager, he attended a meeting in Baltimore. A group of us went to dinner at a local restaurant. Earl Thompson, our New York Regional Manager, went to the men's room. Sharman walked over, picked up the maitre d's microphone, and yelled through the restaurant three times, "Will Earl Thompson please come out of the men's room."

Sharman was designated to pay the check that night, and when the French waiter came, Bob gave him a credit card. The waiter took it but returned to ask if Bob had another card also. Sharman stepped up his voice pitch so that everyone in the restaurant could hear and demanded to know why another card was necessary. The waiter, with a strong French accent said, "Monsieur, we just need something for further identification."

Sharman, yelling now, said, "Oh! It's identification you need, is it? I'll show you identification!" – and with that stood on top of his chair and proceeded to pull his zipper down.

The waiter panicked. His arms flew up, and now he was yelling, "Oh, no, no! It will be all right. Please sit down."

Bob tells one on himself:

> One nice summer day I was riding with a salesman out of Austin, Texas. This was before our cars had air conditioning. We were going down a two-lane country road enjoying the fresh air when he decided to pass a cattle truck just ahead. As we got amidships, one of the cows let loose with a load that hit our windshield and darn near

wrecked the car. I turned to the guy and said that had we been one second sooner, I would have gotten the whole mess in my lap. He looked at me and said, "Mr. Sharman, down here in Texas, when we pass a cattle truck, we roll up our windows." A lesson well learned.

And learn it he did. This story is from Red Elliott:

When Bob Sharman was promoted to Regional Manager in Dallas, Texas, I was promoted to his job as District Sales Manager in Miami, Florida. One day Bob was going to make a few calls with me to introduce me to the Miami retail market. We parked the car at the first call and Bob told me to roll my window up; it could rain at any time in Miami. I replied, "It's too hot to roll up the windows," so I left my side down. Nothing happened. At the second call, we parked the car and Bob told me, "Roll up your window; it could rain at any time in Miami." I again replied, "It's too hot to roll up the windows." When we returned to the car, it had rained very hard for about ten minutes, and the driver's side (my side) was full of water. Bob Sharman said to me, "Sit in it, you dumb son-of-a-b – –, you deserve to have a wet a – –."

Regional Manager, Sharman invited me to Memphis to visit one of our very fine customers, Malone and Hyde. We called on Merchandising Manager Johnny Saviori, a robust but cherubic-looking man with a great sense of humor and an appetite for fun. After about a two-minute interview, John suggested that we depart for the "Monkey Wrench Club." As if by magic, members of Malone and Hyde management and several brokers appeared. Suddenly we were off to this Monkey Wrench Club.

It was a small building owned by Malone and Hyde and was about the size of two side-by-side truck trailers. It contained two areas. The front was occupied by a large round poker table, where big glasses of spirits were served. In the rear was a rub-down table. The same attendant served the drinks and gave the massages. What a way to spend an afternoon – drink and yell and play cards, then get a wonderful, relaxing rubdown, then return to the fray again!

After dinner and a late night, we called on other customers the next morning. About noon, Sharman called John Saviori and was directed to host a follow-up "session" at our hotel room. Within forty-five minutes, we were all drinking again. After several hours of this, I announced that I had to catch the last plane to Baltimore because the shareholders' meeting was the next day.

Johnny Saviori asked Sharman how Malone and Hyde ranked in his region just as I stood up with suitcase in hand to depart this wonderful camaraderie. Sharman lied and said, "You're number one" (actually they were number two.)

Saviori yelled, "Number one?" and said to me, *"Sit down!"* After sitting down, I explained that my boss, Jim Welsh, a non-drinking man, was not going to understand this. Saviori said, "Sharman, get Mr. Welsh on the telephone. We'll take care of this."

Jim Welsh was in President John Curlett's office when he was paged. We had to wait for him to travel the length of the Light Street building to get to his own phone. When he answered, John Saviori said, "Mr. Welsh, this is John Saviori, Vice President of Malone and Hyde, one of your biggest customers. We have a problem down here. Buzz McCormick is drunk and passed out on the floor, and he won't be back in time for the shareholders' meeting." Then he hung up.

With great trepidation I returned to the Company (after just barely making my flight), only to be greeted by a smiling Jim Welsh, who said, "I wish we had that kind of relationship with all our customers."

Years later, our largest grocery customer, Fleming, acquired Malone and Hyde and one of those rascals from the "Monkey Wrench Club," John Moll, was elected President of the entire company. A great storyteller and enthusiastic leader, John is living proof that "hell-raisers" can – and do – win!

Here's another that Sharman tells on himself:

This one involved Hugh McCormick, who was not a drinking man in those days. I was on the task force opening the Detroit market. I drew Hugh McCormick as a room partner. A bunch of us discovered a night club over in

Windsor, Canada, where we went several times that week. It was a nice place with top entertainment.

At the end of the week I was totaling up my expenses and, much to my dismay, discovered that I had spent over $120, which was a lot of dough those days. I asked Hugh how much he had spent and he told me $38. I asked how in the hell could he live all week on thirty-eight bucks. He said it was easy. So, being desperate, I asked Hugh to pick up part of my tab. He was insulted.

As soon as we got back to the office, Hugh went hot-footing up to C. P. to tell him what I tried to do. Sure enough, I got the call to the front office. C.P. started to chew me out, but started laughing so hard he couldn't finish. As a matter of fact, C.P. offered me fifty bucks if I could get Hugh out for a night on the town. I never did.

The favorite vacation spot in Florida for McCormick people for many years was the Daytona Plaza in Daytona Beach.

Dr. Brantley Watson, Vice President - Human Relations, arrived one weekday morning needing a haircut. He went down to the hotel barber shop. There sitting in the chair getting a shave was none other than Florida District Sales Manager Bob Sharman. Sharman was always quick. Seeing Brantley, he jumped up out of the barber chair, stuck out his hand and said, "There you are, Brantley. I've been looking all over the hotel for you to welcome you to Florida."

The last story I'll tell about Bob involves both of us. We were traveling together in North Carolina and spent an evening in Greensboro. Bob took me to a dinner club that he had been told about. The place was beautiful. It was beautifully decorated and had a large bandstand with an eight-piece orchestra for entertainment. The food was excellent, and the crowd was enjoying it. People were dancing to the music.

After dinner, at about ten o'clock, the band took a break. Sharman said to me, "You can play the trumpet. Let's go up on stage and play a little music." We did. I grabbed the trumpet and Bob sat down at the drums (which I don't think he had ever played before), and we started playing some Dixieland tunes. As terrible as it must have sounded, couples came out on the dance floor and were jitterbugging.

But it didn't last long. The bandleader came running out and stopped us. Sharman said, "Look, the people love us," but the bandleader didn't buy it. Instead of saying, "Get off the stage, you bums," he said, "You can't play because you're not in the Union!"

So we sat down and listened to another set. When that set was over, the band retired again. Some people at a nearby table egged us to try again – and again we did. I blew the horn, Sharman banged on the drums, and people danced. This time, however, we were ejected bodily from the nightclub, amid cheers from the crowd. Another free dinner!

The most bizarre thing that I have ever witnessed with any of our people happened in Atlanta. During a sales meeting we all went to dinner in another restaurant that also had a band. The small bandstand stood right in front of the men's room. Win Butz, an account executive at our ad agency, Lennen and Newell, excused himself to go to the bathroom. Not suffering from any shortage of alcohol at the time, Win tripped as he departed the men's room on his return. The band was not playing at the time. As Win continued to fall forward, his head drove right through the bass drum, and he did an unsolicited "Porky Pig" salute. Guess who yelled, "That's all, folks!"

Musical instruments can be dangerous. Clayton Shelhoss, while still a Schilling executive, took several of us to a restaurant in San Francisco's Chinatown. The piano player was a serious fellow with a big scraggly gray beard and a turban on his head – not a friendly type at all.

Clayton is a talented piano player. There is only one problem – he only knows one song! But strangers don't know that, and Clayton plays a wonderful, melodious rendition of "Clair de Lune." He puts feeling into every note and expresses ecstasy in his eyes.

When our turbaned friend took a break, Clayton was encouraged to treat the restaurant owners to "Clair de Lune."

Clayton obliged, but in just a few bars an irate piano player rushed out from behind the curtains and told Clayton to "knock it off." The piano player then disappeared again behind the curtains.

Clayton waited for perhaps a minute and then proceeded to finish his song. But immediately the curtains parted behind Clayton, and a now furious piano player stormed up to the piano and – whack! – threw the keyboard cover down on Clayton's fingers. Clayton reacted just fast enough to clear all ten fingers. To my knowledge, Clayton Shelhoss has never performed in public since.

CHARLES "CHUCK" IRELAND and
JULIAN "CHAMP" BOYER

Chuck Ireland is not only a great wit but has that something extra that few people have – the ability to really "put someone on" with a serious face, making up outrageous lies and never bothering to set the record straight.

In answer to where his wife Mary was, Chuck would usually respond with something like, "Oh, she's out driving the cab tonight." Once, I overheard him at a public party when someone he had just met asked him if his wife was there. He said, "Yes, Mary is right over there," and pointed to a huge, terrible-looking woman who looked like she belonged in a cage.

John Doub was General Manager of the McCormick Division and eventually became Vice President - Purchasing for the Corporation. John and his wife, Margaret, were prototype all-American, family people, and John was conservative enough never to let his hair grow long as the styles changed in the 1960s.

Chuck was introduced to some friends of the Doubs at a cock-tail party. When Chuck found the connection he said, "Isn't that something about John." The couple looked concerned and said, "We don't know. What has happened?" Chuck says, "Oh, you haven't seen him in a while?" They replied that they hadn't. "You didn't know that he has divorced Margaret?" said Chuck. "No-o," was their reply. "Oh, yes. He's drinking a lot and has grown his hair long and is sporting a mustache," Chuck said. "Not John!" they said. "Yes, and he got a vasectomy," said Chuck. Then Chuck walked away to entertain someone else.

Chuck Ireland was a fabled storyteller.

Dave Michels, former General Manager of the McCormick/Schilling Division, tells this story:

This involves Chuck Ireland at the FMI Convention at McCormick Place in Chicago. We had come out of McCormick Place at the end of the day and were going to Chuck's car, which was on the lot next door to the hall. As Chuck opened his door, another car came up from behind him and hit his door. Both hinges were broken off, and the door fell to the ground. Obviously, he could not put the door back in its normal place. With that, he opened the trunk of his car and put the door in the trunk.

We had to drive from McCormick Place up to the Ambassador West Hotel, where we were staying. In the middle of the evening in Chicago Loop rush traffic, we were in the car with no door!

Clark Barrett, "the elitist," was sitting in the back seat and said he was very embarrassed to see that he had to ride around Chicago in this kind of a damaged vehicle and hoped nobody saw him.

Chuck Ireland didn't help matters much when he pulled up next to a car with two elderly lady passengers at a traffic light. As they looked over, Chuck looked at them and made a motion to pull a make-believe blind down between him and the car beside him. They were looking and didn't know whether they should laugh or call a cop.

If that wasn't enough, at the next stop sign, the same ladies drove next to us. This time Chuck Ireland put his leg out onto the street as his car came to a stop. It looked like a kid stopping a coaster. With that both ladies broke out laughing and realized that the man driving the car beside them was slightly crazed.

When he arrived at the hotel, two attendants approached. One opened the door on the right, and the other almost hit Chuck as he grasped for "no door." Everyone laughed except Barrett, who said, "Let me out of this vehicle. This has been the most embarrassing encounter I have ever endured in my life."

Milt van den Berg, Vice President - Planning, ran into Chuck one morning as Chuck was going into a Towson barber shop. Surprised to see Chuck, Milt asked, "What are you doing here?" Chuck, never at a loss for words, said very slowly, "The hair grew on Company time, and I'm getting it cut on Company time."

And another reminder from Dave Michels:

This incident involved Chuck Ireland and one Buzz McCormick. Years ago, the entertainer at the Sand Bar in Ocean City, Maryland was Dick Rheil. As you may recall,

Dick played the piano and engaged in quick banter back and forth with everyone in the bar. Part of his act was, of course, to talk people down and tell quick, one-line stories to his audience.

One evening, Buzz and Chuck came into the Sand Bar, and the idea was to have Chuck Ireland, who was known for his pretty fast comeback and quick wit, to get into some type of a conversation with Dick Rheil. At the break, Dick came over to the table where Chuck had just been seated. Buzz wanted to introduce him to Dick and said, "Dick, I'd like you to meet Chuck Ireland." With that, Chuck started to stand up and Dick said, "Sit down, you don't have to stand up to be introduced to me." Chuck said, "I wasn't standing up to be introduced to you. I have a colostomy and I was adjusting my bag." With that, Dick shot right back and said, "Well, thank God, I thought it was your breath."

Chuck could also be serious on occasion. After dinner at my son Chip's wedding rehearsal at The Hunt Valley Inn, people were starting to look at each other a little bit. I excused myself to go to the men's room, where I found Chuck, who was attending a business dinner. I said, "Chuck, we need an after-dinner speaker. How about following me back to our room?" Chuck did, and I introduced him to the group. He made about a twenty-minute presentation that was absolutely perfect for the occasion. Totally serious and a great message for all the young people.

Chuck obviously enjoys telling stories about others, and here are some from his collection. He loves to talk about Julian "Champ" Boyer, who represented McCormick in Chicago for many years as both Regional Manager and later as National Accounts Manager:

Champ was a large man, originally from Orange, Virginia, where he always wanted to return and retire . . . and did. He used to sweat profusely and changed his clothes frequently on a hot summer day. He was careful never to overexert himself. For instance, when he moved to Pittsburgh and had a house with a small lawn, his wife cut it! According to Chuck . . .

Bud Weiser was giving us a stern lecture at a sales meeting and saying we should be getting more of the egg dye business with our food colors at Easter. He told Boyer he was lazy, and if he would use his contacts with key chain executives in the Midwest, he could get a lot of this business. Champ's response: "Well, Bud, you have to look at the Sta-Sticks-Kits, for most accounts out here sell *brown eggs* and it limits our market for egg dyeing."

Champ and his wife lived in an apartment on the North Side of Chicago. They had a parakeet named "Little Bird." One evening when Bud Weiser and Carter Parkinson were in town, my wife and I were invited to join everyone for dinner at the Boyers. Little Bird was active at the party, in free flight all over the apartment. Parkinson objected to this and insisted the animal be caged. Before Champ obliged, Little Bird swooped in and landed on Parkinson's bald head. Champ's response was that he had told the bird they were having some big shots in that night and to get closer with the Company's key executives. "I guess he took me too seriously."

About every two years we each had a counseling session with RH&R representatives. We arrived for a marketing meeting and a schedule of time was given to all of us. Champ was scheduled right after me. He said, "Chuck, I don't like these shrinks. They make me nervous." He said, "There is a lunch break after your appointment. I want us to have lunch together, and I'd like for you to tell me what goes on."

I had my session, came down, and Champ and I sat together for lunch. I said, "This session was really tough! First of all they talk about your health, family, and how you like your area. Next they want you to answer some tough questions on a product quiz. Next an assistant comes into the room and he wires you up, all over, with a lie-detector machine. Then they wheel in a big red light on a pole and put a tape recorder on the table. You are then given a written quiz on product use, true or false, and you are graded on accuracy and speed. An incorrect answer causes the light to go on. But don't worry. I've taken it before, and every third question is false. Next they ask if you have ever lied on your expense account. If the light goes on, you are asked how many times and what was the largest amount. You are then disconnected from the machine and asked to write a short response of the one thing you admire and the three things you detest about your immediate supervisor."

When he came back, he said to me. "Chuck, I didn't have *any* of those things you told me went on."

Champ was not too energetic and was prone to twist the English language in his oral definitions of certain events. He went out to work one day with one of our young salesmen on a new store set-up. It was in Chicago. The temperature was about 95 degrees, with no air conditioning and a lot of manual assembly of spice racks and heavy boxes of product to handle.

I met our new sales representative the next morning and asked how he enjoyed his day with Mr. Boyer. His response: "He is a great guy. We worked until about 2:00 P.M., and he said for me to take him back to his air conditioned hotel, for Charlie McCormick didn't expect us to work so hard in this blazing hot weather. We played gin rummy and drank gin and tonics."

I also knew Champ well, having reported to him at age 19 in Chicago. Bud Weiser, Vice President - Sales and Marketing, loved Champ as a character, but Champ could drive Weiser nearly insane with his laziness. He lasted thirty years with the Company and was under the "whip" the entire time.

The Chicago office was a two-room office with four desks and a table. Boyer would get frustrated when he would call Weiser only to be told, "I'm sorry, Mr. Weiser is in the Tea House." So in the summer of 1947, Champ ordered out a big green institutional McCormick teapot with the big "Mc" on it and told his secretary to make iced tea for the office. He told me on the day that the teapot arrived, "The next time Bernardo calls [Bud's real first name was Bernard], I'm instructing my secretary to say, 'I'm sorry, Mr. Boyer is having tea in the other office.'" Champ never told me what Bud said, but the next time I went into the office, the teapot was gone and never mentioned again!

Incidentally, Champ is the only person ever to be married in the Tea House. He did very much love the Company.

More from Chuck Ireland:

> The ingenuity of McCormick salesmen never ceased to amuse me. They not only loved their work, they also had fun doing it. One of the boys who had a Brooklyn territory related this incident from a hot day in July. The supply of pepper was tighter than anything on his list. He made a promise to a good customer that he would find some pepper somewhere for him before he came again. The search for this commodity during the war years was hopeless.
>
> He realized on the day of his planned visit that he could not deliver, and the merchant was sure to scream at him, to say the least. So he said to his adolescent son, "I need your big woolly earmuffs." "But Dad," the boy replied, "it's the middle of July." "Don't give me a hard time," the father said, "just bring me the earmuffs." The earmuffs were produced, and the salesman took off to call on his client. When he arrived at the door of his store, he pulled out the earmuffs and put them on. He walked into the store and said to the owner, "All right, give me hell! I didn't get your pepper." They both broke out into a hearty laugh. The promise was forgiven, and the client was retained.
>
> On another occasion, Bud Roth and Carl Holmes were on an overnight trip to Scranton, Pennsylvania. They had had two tough calls that morning and were proceeding home, south on Route 81. The only place on that stretch was a restaurant called "Top of the 80's" at the intersection of Routes 80 and 81. They were relaxing, celebrating a successful trip with martinis. They had just ordered another round when, as the story goes, Carl Holmes, who was facing the door, turned every color of the rainbow. Their bosses, Bob Crampton and Dave Michels, walked in, returning from the west on Route 80. They too found the only place for a light lunch was "Top of the 80's."
>
> A stern lecture ensued about drinking at lunch without the presence of a customer, which was a strict Company taboo. Odds of that happening had to be millions to one!

CLARK BARRETT

Clark makes our all-time McCormick character team because of his gentlemanliness and his abhorrence of embarrassment. Having been schooled at both the Gilman School and Dartmouth College, "Clarkie," as he refers to himself, always appeared to be the only blueblood in the McCormick sales organization.

Now we have had other Dartmouth graduates, but none has ever seemed to be so embellished with charm. He twice, for lengthy periods of time, reported to gentlemen who were not members of the Board of Directors. Clarkie was a member, having been elected at a young age, and that alone made for great conversation.

We were attending a supermarket convention in Miami, Florida and staying at the Fountainebleau Hotel. Five of us picked up Schilling Regional Manager Mel Appling at the airport

(l-r): Brantley Watson, Clark Barrett, Paul Frisch.

and went out to relax for the evening. Upon returning, Clark was driving, and just as we approached the hotel he dropped his cigarette down between the seat and the car door. He took his foot off the accelerator, opened the door slightly, and reached down. The car slowed to about 5 m.p.h. and went slightly to the right. Big red and blue lights flashed behind us and we halted.

One policeman stayed in the squad car while the other came forward. He shined his flashlight in at Clark and said, "Pull over to the side." Then as he saw Clark's red face, he said, "On second thought, don't move." He took Clark back to the squad car for what seemed a long time.

Mel Appling, who hadn't had a drink said, "I'd better go back and help ol' Clarkie out." Mel walked back to the squad car, where the cops told him to get lost. But his straightforwardness had made its mark. When the officer finally came back with Clark, he flashed his light on all of us. We looked okay because nobody gets as red as Clark does. Indignantly, the officer said, "I don't understand why the only drunk guy in the car is driving." We said, "It's because he's the boss."

The officer said, "Well, anybody can drive this car to the hotel parking lot but him." In reality, Clark hadn't had any more to drink than anyone else except Appling. He just looked that way. In his own words, he once again was "mortified."

In Atlantic City while attending a Supermarket Institute Convention, Clark once brought a guy into our suite who was obviously inebriated. But he had met him coming up on the elevator and with his usual graciousness and charm invited him in. Clark introduced him as Bill Brandt. Someone said, "No kidding, we have a Bill Brandt in our Company" (our Bill Brandt, being CFO of SETCO). The guest mumbled, "Izzat right? Wha's his name?" We threw him out of the room, and Clark was embarrassed again.

Some McCormick sales executives were entertaining down on Baltimore's famous "Block" at the Oasis Club. During the course of the evening one of the dancing girls, named "Zorro," who did a striptease out of an appropriate black outfit, exclaimed, "McCormick? Do you know Clarkie boy?"

Clark, who was a bachelor for fifty-seven years, had entertained many customers on the Block and knew many of the characters. One of our guys said, "Certainly we know Clark, but how do you know Clark?" Zorro said, "Clarkie is the best there is in this town." The next morning at the round table in back of the Tea House the story spread fast, and everyone waited for Clark to appear. When he did and heard the story, he smiled and shrugged it off with, "How about that, a testimonial from a hooker!"

And another Barrett story from Dave Michels:

> This involves Clark Barrett at a trade conference in Acapulco. I was there with Clark. We were having a presentation from an author who had just written a book about corporate structure and behavior. While Clark and I were attending this conference, we were sitting under an air conditioning vent, which was blowing directly down on us. About three rows behind were all of the Campbell Soup characters, such as Harry Sanner, Frank McGuinness, and Jim McNutt. As the author got to the point of his presentation, explaining some of the problems with American industry, he stated that one of the most prevalent problems was that the "majority of key executives in the United States take early retirement while failing to inform the company."
>
> Just at that time, Clark said that he had enough of the direct air conditioning blowing on him, stood up and started to the back of the room, at which time one of the Campbell people exclaimed, "Clark, don't take what he said personally!" Needless to say, the entire room roared. Clark was rather red-faced as he found his way out.

One year, Clark Barrett, Dave Michels, Jack Loomis, and I were having dinner at the Pen and Pencil Restaurant in Atlantic City during the FMI (Food Marketing Institute) convention. Loomis had just joined the Company, and Schilling had sent him east to meet some of the McCormick salesmen and to attend the convention. Dave Michels was McCormick's Vice President of Sales and Marketing, and reporting to him was Clark, who was also on the McCormick Board of Directors. Dave wasn't. It had been a long stand-up cocktail hour after a hard day on our feet at the convention.

Waiting for dinner we had several more drinks, and mouths were moving more rapidly. Michels got on his favorite subject, "the corporates." He said, "If it weren't for the heavy burden of the corporate staff, we'd have more money to compete with." I countered with, "If there weren't any corporation, there wouldn't be any divisions." (Being a corporate staffer myself, I had to get into the contest.) Michels then exploded and heaped all his wrath on the corporate hierarchy.

Clark ended it all with this comment to his boss: "Davey boy, if you don't like it, get the #!!@!! out." Dave was so mad he couldn't talk. Just a little stammering came out – and Loomie's eyes got bigger and bigger with amazement.

Here's a finale on Clark as told by Distribution Manager John Highfield:

> A few years ago, shortly after his retirement, Clark Barrett was asked by Dave Michels to join him on a very important call. An old and dear friend of Clark's from the Red Coats golf group, and the top man for our customer, was extremely unhappy with McCormick & Company. He was about to throw us out of the account. Carter Parkinson was still at the Company at the time and in charge of the entire consumer group. Clark agreed to make the call with Dave. Between them they were able to salvage the account – no small achievement under the very serious circumstances.
>
> Prior to departing, Clark mentioned to his long-time friend George Franke that he was taking the trip with Dave and gave George a few details. The message was clear that this was a very important undertaking.
>
> George is an old-line Baltimore guy, successfully retired and Clark's contemporary. He has always been interested in McCormick. He knew Dave Michels and knew Carter Parkinson even better, since they were both members of the Baltimore Country Club.
>
> George has a sharp tongue and quick wit and had always delighted in putting the needle into Carter. When Clark got back to Baltimore, George asked Clark how the

trip had gone, and Clark said that it had been a great success.

The very next evening, George sauntered into the men's bar at the in-town Baltimore Country Club, as was his custom. There was the usual gathering of members when George walked in, and Carter Parkinson was firmly ensconced in his favorite spot at the bar, holding forth as he was so often known to do.

This seemed to George a perfect opportunity to once again stick the needle into Parkinson. George has never been one to miss such an opportunity. He remarked, "Well, I see they had to bring out the old war horse to save McCormick's biggest account! Clark Barrett had to come out of retirement to come to the rescue!" George went on from there, detailing all the particulars, while Parkinson practically choked on his martini – embarrassed. He was furious at George, but even more furious at Clark. George ran with the ball for most of the rest of the cocktail hour, stealing center stage from Parkinson and rubbing salt into the wound.

The next day, Clark went to Light Street to meet with Dave Michels to review their meeting and prepare a follow-up letter. As Clark walked down the hall, he passed Parkinson's office. As he passed the door, he heard a bellow: "Barrett, get your a – – in here! You S.O.B., telling that loudmouth George Franke that story and embarrassing me in front of all my friends! I ought to punch you in the mouth!" Very cooly, Barrett said, "Carter, I don't work for you any more. I did a favor for Dave and McCormick. I'll tell George Franke any damn thing I want, and if you dare to come out from behind that desk, I'll knock you through that #!!@!! window."

(Parkinson had the office on the seventh floor just to the left of the receptionist's desk, and it had a beautiful, big window overlooking the harbor.) Parkinson stayed right where he was, never said another word, and Barrett turned and walked on to his meeting with Dave Michels.

EDWARD J. VINNECOMBE

If Ed Vinnecombe had been born into a circus family, he

would have quickly gravitated to the patent-medicine booth, where he would have become the greatest pitch-man of all time. The prototype builder of "molehills" into "mountains," Vinnecombe has an emotional conviction to a wide variety of subjects. He came to love McCormick shortly after World War II. On many occasions after that, one might have thought that Ed was capable of starting World War III.

The first time I met Ed was at C.P.'s house. Ed was a Lieutenant Colonel in the U.S. Army and responsible for the Women's Army Corps in the 3rd Service Command. C.P. was proud that the Company had just won its second Army-Navy E award for service to the military. With great flourish, Ed was addressing the guests, and particularly C.P., down in C.P.'s clubroom, stating what a great accomplishment this was and that it must be celebrated in a style commensurate with its achievement. He said, "Charlie, we'll reserve the 5th Regiment Armory, and we'll fill it up with people. We'll bring in the Women's Army Corps, and we'll parade those WACs up and down the armory. It will be a hell of a thing."

Ed whipped the guests into a near frenzy with the excitement of parading all the women back and forth in honor of McCormick. Of course it never happened, but that is beside the point. Meanwhile, upstairs in the kitchen, Colonel Vinnecombe's Army Sergeant driver was pacing back and forth beside a cook, who was carrying a plate of food from which he was snacking – while casting an eye at the hallway door. Someone asked the sergeant why he didn't just sit down and enjoy some food, and he replied, "If Colonel Vinnecombe saw me eating while on duty, he would cut my arm off."

Ed joined the Company after the war and started up the Bulk and Institutional Division, became a master tea-taster, and ultimately Vice President of Corporate Communications, the position that a circus atmosphere might well have trained him for.

Some of Ed's convictions were quite logical. "When buying a mattress, buy the best because you will spend one-third of your life on it."

During the Korean War, the price of pepper went sky-high –

Ed Vinnecombe was always a one-man Barnum and Bailey show.

over three dollars a pound. We went to the famous Haussner's Restaurant in old East Baltimore for lunch, and Ed was appalled to see imitation pepper in the pepper shakers.

He immediately asked to see the owner, who came out of the kitchen to visit us. Ed said, "Look, if you need to save money, do it back in the kitchen, not out here on the table where everyone can see it." Haussner had to agree.

Edward was not only emotional, but very excitable. He was visiting the Schilling Division in San Francisco in 1957. While he was on a telephone call to Baltimore, a small earthquake hit the area. Ed screamed over the phone, "We're having an earthquake!" and abruptly hung up. The phone lines to the East were then cut off for a number of hours. Folks in Baltimore envisioned a great catastrophe. As it turned out, there was no real damage to speak of.

Ed's office was on Friendship Court right across from the Tea House. This was perfect for Ed because it was a high-traffic area, and Ed liked to patrol the floor. He particularly liked to impress visiting guests. Vinnecombe is an unusual name and a tough one to remember. One day, one of the reception hostesses was overheard as she addressed a new recruit. She said, "If a stranger arrives with no specific appointment, call on Mr. Benny Cohen."

And here's another name twister as related by Paul Irwin:

> Back in the late 1950s, Dick Hall, our Vice President of Research and Development, undertook a special project on a new process for making instant tea. The specialist who brought this process opportunity to McCormick and was hired as a consultant was a gentleman named Mike Bonato. Ed Vinnecombe, who was then our Vice President of the Institutional Division, was a real charger in terms of bringing customers and others into the Light Street building and introducing them to various people in our Company. Ed enjoyed dramatizing each of his day's events, and visitors thoroughly enjoyed his tours.
>
> I was in the entrance of the building with some visitors as Mike Bonato entered from a side door. Now Ed had never quite gotten the pronunciation of Mike Bonato's name correct and continually referred to him as "Mike Bonito." On this occasion, Ed once again introduced the visitors to "Mike Bonito." Finally, Mike, in a rage overheard by all, muttered, "When is that man going to realize I am not a tuna fish. If he doesn't stop screwing up my name, I'm going to call him Mr. Honeycomb."

Ed visited India while he held responsibility for the tea department. One of the relics he brought back with him was an Indian flute. One tour group walking up Friendship Court was interrupted by Ed, who charged out of his office blowing on the flute and marched through the group like the pied piper.

When he was forced to have a hemorrhoid operation, rather than being embarrassed about the inner-tube cushion that he sat on for weeks afterward, Edward proudly carried it around with him like a Purple Heart badge of honor or something. Later, suffering from ulcers, he carried a luxurious leather bag with shoulder strap. When he heard a tour group outside his office, he would dash out into the unsuspecting group with the comment, "Ladies, in this bag are all the necessary remedies for a bleeding ulcer."

We went away on a week's vacation to Cape Cod with Ed and his wife, Sylvia. After arriving at our rented house, Ed called the local social clubs, introduced himself, and let them know that he had just returned from India and would be pleased to show his films and perform as a speaker for their weekly lunch.

While visiting Schilling, Ed held a briefing on a subject that should have involved three or four people at most. R.C. Crampton, General Manager, was annoyed when the entire executive staff seemed to be missing one morning, and he couldn't find anyone to talk to. He searched the area and finally opened a door to the boardroom to find everyone sitting in there spellbound by Vinnecombe, who had rounded up a large enough group to be worthy of his "major pitch." Ed had to have an audience.

Ed is one of the few people who remember the details of the Schilling acquisition in 1947.

> After C.P. told the Baltimore banks he would be damned if he would hand them control of the Company, the directors were asked to invest in McCormick stock to the extent possible. We were still short of funds when our Treasurer, Brooke Furr, traveled to San Francisco. In a most elated phone call, he stated that the funding problem was solved. Schilling was in the coffee business and had a five-year contract with coffee brokers. The market jumped from 23¢ to $1.00 a pound, and the brokers were all sweating. They were happy to lend us money in return for letting them off the hook on their five-year contract.

KEENE ROADMAN

Keene Roadman met C.P. in Geneva, Switzerland while working in the Bureau of Labor Statistics for the U.S. Labor Department. C.P. was the U.S. employer delegate to the International Labor Organization's conference. Keene joined the Company as our first market researcher. One of his early projects was a program for routing our salesmen on their territories, thus earning him the nickname "Roadman the routeman."

One of Keene's characteristics was that he never knew or cared what time it was, nor really what day it was. Chuck Mattern, Advertising Manager, was talking with New York one morning, and our agency account executive stated that he was expecting Keene to arrive in just a few minutes. Chuck said, "That's odd, Keene just passed by my office." Roadman had merely forgotten what day it was. More evenings than not, Roadman would call up his wife, Dawn, about 9:00 or 10:00 P.M. and say, "Dawn, honey, I'm going to be a little late for dinner." She would say, "OK," without being the least bit surprised or irritated.

While vacationing in Daytona Beach one year, Keene slipped on wet cement and broke his wrist. He was quite annoyed that he couldn't participate in normal vacation events like swimming or golfing. So he peroxided his hair for lack of other entertainment and returned to the office with "orange" hair. The secretaries were equally divided as to whether he looked better or worse.

Subconsciously, Roadman enjoyed needling Carter Parkinson. Carter was a handsome man, but without hair on top. At a New Orleans regional sales meeting, Keene addressed the group by saying, "I know you all wonder how we come up with our sales projections. Actually it's very simple. We shine a bright light on Carter's head and read it like a crystal ball!" Carter, who was Vice President of Sales and Marketing, didn't appreciate it a bit.

That evening was a late one for all the troops – a night out on the town in New Orleans. At 2:30 in the morning we ended up in the "morning call" coffee house. Roadman ended up with his arm around a complete stranger, singing "Down by the Riverside." Parkinson, who was tired by now and wanted to go home, ridiculed Roadman for his exuberance until he found out that Keene's newfound friend worked at Super Valu – a very major customer.

Roadman made Parkinson absolutely furious again at an Atlanta sales meeting dinner. Unbeknownst to Roadman, the next day was to be a demotion day for our District Manager, Bob Caldwell. Bob was an old-time employee, and Carter was not looking forward to giving him the word. At the end of the dinner, Roadman, feeling that Carter had not injected enough joviality or speeches for a sales dinner, rose and addressed the group. As Carter's face reddened with anger, Roadman conducted a testimonial for good ol' Bob Caldwell and the great job he did in leading the Atlanta sales force. Carter kept trying to shut Roadman up, but he just couldn't be stopped. It was a disaster!

Roadman had an old Dodge convertible that five of us used to carpool in. One night on the way home from work, we ran out of gas in downtown Baltimore. We pushed the car uphill for three blocks into a gas station. The attendant came out, and to all of our amazement, Roadman instructed him to put 50¢ worth of gas in the car, saying that was enough to get him home.

That story is only topped by one on Bud Roth, Baltimore Regional Manager. After a local dinner in Hunt Valley, Roth was driving home Fred Ogburn, Human Relations Manager. Fred had limited vision and couldn't drive. On this evening it seems Roth had little vision too. After entering the car and starting the engine, Bud said to Fred, "My gas tank is empty. I'll have to stop at the filling station." Driving down to the nearest gas station, Bud asked the attendant to fill the tank. The attendant put the nozzle in the gas tank and announced that no fuel would pump because "your tank is full." Roth read his gasoline gauge again, now realizing that he had read it backwards!

One day before Keene broke his wrist in Daytona Beach, he observed that there were some elderly ladies sitting around the swimming pool. Keene thought they could stand a little entertainment, so he put on his wife's bathing suit, stuffed it with grapefruits, put on a bathing cap and went to the pool area. He walked around the pool once and then climbed the high dive. He proceeded to sit on the end of the diving board while reading a newspaper.

The ladies were in awe of this strange-looking woman, sitting on the end of the board. When a waiter, dressed in a red jacket and black pants, appeared with a tall drink on his tray and yelled, "Who ordered this drink?" Roadman signaled from the diving board, and the waiter climbed the stairs with the drink balanced on a tray. As he approached Roadman he tripped over him and Roadman, the waiter, the tray, and the drink went into the pool. The ladies were aghast and didn't realize what had really happened until up floated the waiter, Roadman, and the two grapefruits!

Keene Roadman did a most humane thing one night after the annual Advertising Club of Baltimore banquet. Out in front of the old Emerson Hotel we were approached by a young bum who wanted a quarter for a cup of coffee. Roadman felt sorry for him because it was so cold out. So rather than giving the bum a quarter, Keene gave him his hat. The man was so appreciative and happy that Keene then took off his overcoat and put it on the bum. The "pièce de résistance" came when Keene realized that he was left with a white silk scarf around his neck, which he promptly draped on his new friend, thus completing his outfit. I don't know who was happier, Roadman or the bum!

After Roadman gave away his overcoat, he never owned one again. He repeatedly caught pneumonia, and eventually died of it.

LOUIS V. TOWT

Louie Towt joined the Company after developing a process for the quick curing of vanilla beans. Instead of the usual method of alternately drying the beans in the sun by day and storing to sweat by night (a process that took months), Louis's process took only forty-eight hours. We hired Louis, put his equipment down in Mexico, and cured beans by his process for years until the raw supplies dwindled.

Louie had a great sense of humor and was a very funny guy. He formerly had been a purchasing agent at the Borden Dairy Company in Los Angeles. While there, he turned down a new product idea out of hand.

His boss called him up to his office one afternoon and asked, "Louie, about a year ago did you turn down a new idea for a product called a 'Popsicle'?" Louis thought a moment and said, "As a matter of fact I did." With that, his boss's fist came down on the desk and shattered its glass top into hundreds of pieces.

Louie had a competitor friend in the vanilla business, and when they were together they liked to put on little acts. Louis would rig his shirt just right so that his friend could grab his collar and pull the shirt right off his back without disturbing his suit coat. This was a great convention gag and was very effective in serious restaurants.

Louie used to like to tell two stories: One was about when he was a kid riding on a ferris wheel. As his car was on the downward side of the circle, somebody in the car right above him leaned forward and threw up all over Louie! His other story had to do with a gin rummy game he was watching. Two fellas were playing for big bucks. The game was close and near the end. One player dealt to the other, who laid his hand down without drawing and shouted "Gin!" The dealer rose up out of his chair and threw up on the table.

For several years, Louie spent three months a year running the vanilla operations, which were in a supplier's warehouse in the tiny hillside town of San Luis Acateno, Mexico. There were several bedrooms built above the warehouse off an outside balcony. The butcher shop across the street consisted of one outdoor hook on which a slab of black beef hung. Population was about 200. After about the first two and a half months of the first spring that Louie lived there, the townspeople started to worry about him. A committee came to visit our supplier, Manuel de La Sierra, to voice the town's concern. The gringo had been without a woman for over two months, and they wanted to rectify that.

Manuel told Louie of the town's concern for him, and Louie became concerned himself, and quite rightly so. That afternoon Manuel told Louie to appear on the balcony, which he dutifully did. Down the dirt main street came a parade of the townspeople bringing the town "puta" (prostitute) as a gift for Louie. She was a terrible-looking thing and was suffering from tuberculosis. She was smiling broadly and waving up to Louie on the balcony. Now this had the makings of a real international incident: country culture, business relationship, community politics, sex, and disease. What more could you want? Louie had to think fast, and he did. Remembering back to past tie-breaking achievements, he did the obvious thing and got violently ill! That ended the party.

Louis made his first vacation trip down to Daytona Beach. Roadman and I were ready for him, having announced to local authorities that the Governor of Madagascar was arriving. When Louis stepped off the train in Daytona, he was greeted by the police chief himself and given a personal escort to the hotel.

We had also talked the hotel and hotel band into setting up a special cocktail reception for the celebrity. Louie didn't really know what the hell was going on until he arrived at the hotel, was greeted by the manager, and saw a billboard in the lobby greeting Louis V. Towt, Governor of Madagascar. Louie was then ushered into a private cocktail party in his honor amid joyous music played by the hotel orchestra. We took pictures of Louie before, during, and after the party. He got totally blitzed, to the delight of the gathering.

The hotel photographer took many, many pictures of the event and spent the next week trying to find out who was responsible for the affair and who wanted the pictures and the bill. He sold one set of four pictures. When Brantley Watson, Vice President of Human Relations, arrived a few days later, the photographer had finally caught on to the scam. He was all over Brantley, working on him to tell us to pay for some more pictures. Brantley tried, but of course he failed.

DREW OLE OLSON

There are many others who deserve mention with the elite group above, such as Ole Olson, who was ordering "pink-in-the-middle" steaks way back in the 1940s before most chefs knew the term. Ole always ordered a sirloin steak, pink in the middle, when traveling with other sales executives. The routine was always the same. Ole ordered the steak. The waiter brought the steak. Ole would pick up his knife and fork and cut the steak right down the middle, look into the center, throw his knife and fork down, and exclaim, "It's not pink in the middle." By cutting the steak down the center, Ole, of course, rendered it unsalable to anyone else. Another steak would come out, and chances were that it was the same drill all over again. It was great dinner entertainment for all the dinner partners, and nobody ever knew if Ole just "had" to have the steak that way or if he just enjoyed harassing the restaurant.

DAVE GREEN

Then in modern times there's Dave Green, who moved to Australia to run our plant. When getting his Australian work permit, he was asked if he had any criminal record. Dave replied, "I didn't know one was required anymore."

This is the same Dave Green who set up a little Asian employee who was scheduled to meet with Dr. Jack Gillespie, our Company psychologist from RH&R. Dave instructed the guy to go in the room, take off all his clothes, and wait for the psychologist. Dr. Gillespie was quite surprised to walk in the room and find this little nude fellow waiting for him.

PETE MATTSON

Then there was Pete Mattson, who had almost as much gall as Bob Sharman. Here's what Dallas Regional Manager Joe Harper had to say about him.

> Pete Mattson of the old Schilling Division was a very creative individual who applied this creativity to new products. Bag 'N Season and Taco Casserole were two of his many ideas. Pete was very tall (over 6'5") and had facial features that would not have allowed him to be mistaken for Robert Redford. At one manager meeting, Pete enjoyed his fair share of Beefeaters gin prior to dinner. During dinner Pete disappeared, and in a few minutes we heard a woman scream from the other side of the restaurant. Pete had gone outside, pressed his less than handsome face to the window, and nearly scared the diner to death.
>
> It can be assumed that she did not stay to order dessert and coffee. Pete was ushered back to his seat, where he promptly fell asleep on the shoulder of none other than R.C. Crampton.

Pete was delivering me to the Old Palace Hotel in San Francisco one evening as the rain poured. There was a doorman standing on the upper step to the front door, watching us arrive. At the last second Pete swerved to the right, mounting the curb, the sidewalk, and then the first step as the alarmed doorman barely jumped out of the way. Pete looked at me and said, "Didn't want you to get wet!"

He always looked peculiar driving his Volkswagen bug because he was too big for it. For kicks and some comfort he also used to drive it around with the sunroof open and his head sticking up over the top of the roof. More than one driver almost ran off the road after passing Pete.

I have some other nice tales to tell on Pete, but they're unprintable.

Chapter Eleven

A First Lady Speaks

For any McCormick executive, the support provided by a spouse is much more important than one might presume. The pace of our very competitive business is such that priorities must put business obligations on the top of the list. The family ultimately comes first, but many times "not right now" if one is taking the longer view.

The friendly personalities of McCormick wives have been instrumental in successful customer development through the years. On an indirect basis, of course, family support is vital.

I asked my first lady, Jimi, to collect a few experiences from the traveling spouses' point of view. Here are some of those stories of "wives on the road."

Lois Wells was an honored guest, along with Harry, at a gala dinner in Japan. Course after course was served, building up to the "pièce de résistance." With great ceremony the platter was laid on the table, an exciting and exotic presentation – a freshly filleted fish, which was still breathing! Now this was "fresh" fish – but Lois quickly became allergic to fish.

She was better prepared when they were guests again, this time at the Chinese Embassy in Washington, D.C. Another party, another show, black tie and all the frills. This time, on the way over in the limo, they discussed the copious amount of silverware used at these gala functions. Lois very specifically reminded Harry how to select the proper utensil, by starting at the outside and working his way in. All went well until they were seated at separate tables, and without Lois to instruct him further, Harry found only chopsticks beside his plate! So much for good planning.

Jennefer Thomas has an international collection of ladies' room stories, which only once again proves that travel isn't always as romantic as it sounds. From Paris to Beijing, China, conditions warrant both caution and bravery.

In Paris, Jennefer was carrying around a three-pound piece of chain attached to the key for the hotel safe-deposit box. Having been scalded by the hotel shower, she was unimpressed with her quarters and was looking forward to a nice Paris lunch. Joining two other ladies, all went well until they decided to avail themselves of the ladies' room facilities, which were three stories down in the basement. They were surprised to find three compartments with floor to ceiling doors.

However, after they were individually closed off in what Jennefer describes as a tomb-like area, all the lights went out. After some pangs of panic, followed by much laughter, the three ladies finally groped their way to the entrance door and found the master light switch. The energy conscious restaurateurs had installed a timer on the light switch.

Very effective for return visits.

In China, Jennefer entered an airport ladies' room. It was a large room and, surprisingly, had a private toilet (there usually being nothing but a hole in the ground).

After checking under the door for feet, Jennefer pushed the door open and hit a woman who was *standing* on the seat of the commode. Having caused the lady to lose her balance, Jennefer forgot her need, apologized, and departed.

Donna Lee Frisch would like to forget her moment of truth or embarrassment – whatever. While at a convention in Berlin, Germany, she decided to take a sauna at the hotel spa to relax a bit from the stress of travel.

Looking forward to a quiet moment, she arrived at the sauna, only to learn that it was all nude and co-ed! Oh, well, thought Donna Lee, when in Germany, do as the Germans do. Stepping inside the sauna, adjusting her eyes to the light, she was confronted with the large nude body of a well-known McCormick marketing consultant! "Well hello – and how are you?!!"

Needing a place to hide, Donna Lee jumped up to the highest ledge, where she proceeded to wait until her friend departed. Since they were waiting for each other to leave, this took some time. Anyone who's ever taken a sauna knows that the upper seat is the hottest spot in town, and poor Donna Lee almost perished up there. Finally he left. At the evening cocktail party, he said to her with a grin, "You look great!" When he saw her a year later she was greeted with, "I haven't seen much of you lately!"

Not to play one-upmanship, but while living in California while Buzz was at Setco, I was preparing to entertain customers at home one particular evening. I ran out to the store in L.A. to pick up some last-minute goodies. On the way home down the main drag of Lincoln Boulevard, there was a traffic snarl caused by a firetruck (with all lights blazing but no siren) turning out of a Taco Bell right into my path. I had no choice but to stop and let it go by.

Suddenly I saw why this truck was there. It was accompanying a very tall, wild-looking naked man who proceeded to approach my car, smiling. He leaned on the hood and looked directly into my face. With a small car, top down, this was a little too close.

Looking for help or divine guidance from above, I saw the faces of the firemen, who motioned me not to react. I didn't. The man moved on, wobbling down the street. By this time a helicopter had arrived overhead, dropping a stun gun to subdue the wild man.

I was shaking so badly that I drove into my normal gas station right around the corner to collect my nerves before going home to entertain guests. Knowing the guys in the gas station, I got into this conversation with them:

"What in the #!!@!! is happening on Lincoln – helicopter, police, etc.?" I said, "I don't know, but there's a naked man walking up the middle of the street." One of the guys asked, "Is he a really tall, red-headed guy with a really long – er – ah, beard?" "Well, now that you mention it – ." "Oh, that's just Mike. He must be on PCP again." The real conversation starter for our guests that evening was Mike's buns and Jimi's car on the local news!

Then there was the morning that John McCormick's wife, Wynne, almost panicked. Jumping out of bed after a very early wake-up call, she was dressing still half asleep so she could arrive at the airport in time for the next travel segment, when she made a terrible discovery. Apparently she had a serious nosebleed during the night because her hair was stiff as a board and sticking out at strange angles. En route to the airport, she found brushing useless, and donned a scarf for the day and evening. As she was retiring that night after a stressful day, she discovered what had happened. There had been no nosebleed. The dear lady had merely fallen asleep on the chocolate left on the hotel pillow!

Sweet dreams for sure.

Dorsey Baldwin's wife, Maureen, went to The Hunt Valley Inn to join Dorsey, who was working on New Year's Eve. The Inn was beautifully decorated for the holiday festivities, and filled with men in black ties and ladies in evening dresses. At midnight, Maureen decided to call home and wish the kids a Happy New Year. Just as her call went through, New Year's Eve, Hunt Valley style, erupted as a streaker ran past the telephones, through the main lobby and the Maryland ballroom lobby, and back into the main lobby before he was caught and thrown out the front door into the cold.

Maureen speaks the truth when she says, "Being a McCormick wife involves many diversified tasks." Entertaining customers with Dorsey one evening at The Hunt Valley Inn became quite interesting after a few drinks, a wonderful meal, and a "few" more drinks in the cocktail lounge. All during dinner, the customer and his wife had traded snide remarks. Finally Dorsey interceded, but failed. A few more terse words were spoken and the customer's wife retired to her room in a huff. The customer then suggested that Maureen go retrieve his wife and salvage what was left of a "wonderful" evening.

Being the sport that she is, but with much trepidation, Maureen scooted up to the customer's room and knocked on the door. The woman, totally nude, opened the door while Maureen delivered her message, "We are waiting for you in the lounge!" The nude lady started crying and sat down on the bed, proceeding to give Maureen a running gun-battle description of all her marital problems. This continued for twenty minutes before "the McCormick wife" talked her into redressing and returning to the lounge. You can bet it was a proud moment when she delivered this woman back to more Baldwin late-night entertainment.

But Maureen doesn't discuss her own miff when she called Dorsey at the office to deliver some personal news.

It was after five on a weekday night, and Dorsey and some of the boys were playing a little gin in the Crow's Nest down on Light Street. The phone rang. It was for Dorsey. He laid down his cards, picked up the phone and said, "Yes?" Maureen said: "I've just been to the doctor. I'm pregnant!" There was a pause, after which Dorsey defiantly asked, "Who is this?"

Chapter Twelve

Buzz and Bailey

THE FOCUS YEARS

One Thursday night in February 1987, our phone rang in Laguna Beach, California. At the time I was heading up our packaging group consisting of Setco and Tubed Products.

The caller was Chairman Harry Wells. I had received word earlier that day asking me to be available to take a call from him.

After spending a few minutes on another subject, Harry explained to me that he planned to recommend to the Board of Directors on the following Monday that I be named President and Chief Executive Officer of the Company, and that Bailey Thomas be named Executive Vice President and Chief Operating Officer. Harry said he planned to retire in the fall when I would become Chairman and Bailey, President. He told me our President, Hilly Wilson, also planned to retire.

This came as quite a surprise, even though there had been rumors in recent months that at least four of us were being considered for the top two positions. As a matter of fact, I had been contacted by Jack Thompson, the President of RH&R, our industrial psychologist, some months before, and we had dinner together at The Hunt Valley Inn. Jack was working with Harry on management succession plans and was interested in my perceptions of the future of the Company. Toward the end of dinner, he mentioned that some decisions were going to be made and asked if my "hat was in the ring." I said I didn't know. I hadn't really thought about it and didn't know what the perception was. For many years I had not expected to be considered for such a leadership role.

When I returned to California, I asked my wife, Jimi, to go out and buy the ugliest hat she could find. She bought one, but it wasn't ugly enough. So I went down to the hat store with her and picked out a "Jim Bowie" type, which she mailed to Harry. Enclosed was a little note announcing, "My hat is in the ring."

Harry had a lot of fun with that. He called me and told me that he had received the hat and that I could expect a reply. Several weeks went by before I received an envelope from Harry. In it was a note and a picture. The note said, "I liked the hat so much I decided to keep it." The picture was of Harry wearing the hat! After my election as President of McCormick, we had a management party. Harry told this story and presented the hat to me. It has a place of honor in our home.

The real "hat man," however, is Bailey Thomas, who has the largest collection of hats known to man. One of Bailey's great leadership skills is his ability to dress up in ridiculous costumes at various Company meetings and events.

Before Bailey's election as President, George Clausen, President of Gilroy Foods, talked Bailey into a bet. If George made his budget, Bailey agreed to dress up in any costume Clausen provided. George won and asked Bailey to dress up in a frog suit for the Gilroy Christmas dinner party. During the ceremony, amid music and laughter, Bailey was kissed by a beautiful young lady, then quickly shed the frog suit and turned into a prince. He was well rehearsed. The night before when he tried on the white satin prince costume, Bailey thought it looked so good that he wore it down to the hotel bar to see what the reaction would be. Bailey claims that as a prince he even got offers at the bar!

He chose another costume for a McCormick/Schilling sales meeting when he appeared dressed as a 19th century banker who knew our founder Willoughby. As he talked, he began complaining about how hot the room was. He started taking off parts of his costume until he was transformed into Batman, and dashed out of the room to the strains of the Batman theme song.

Another time, Bailey came as the "world," dressed in a big globe, for an international marketing meeting. The next year,

Bailey Thomas will take on any guise to inspire an audience.

1992, he appeared as Christopher Columbus. This time he was upstaged by his wife, Jennefer, who broke into the room dressed as Columbus's wife. She proceeded to read him the riot act for leaving home to discover new things.

Jim Albrecht, Vice President - International, gives us this Bailey story:

It was one of those Santa Claus occasions. McCormick-Stange Flavor Division was holding its Christmas General Meeting at Oregon Ridge Park. There were several hundred people present, and the room was very warm. Bailey, dressed as Santa, entered the room at the beginning of the meeting, and was scheduled to present C.P. McCormick Awards and make some inspirational year-end remarks toward the end of the meeting.

> At this particular meeting, Bailey was preceded on the program by Gary Zimmerman and Randy Jensen. These gentlemen had a lot to say, especially Jensen. Randy articulated a myriad of operations-related details, preceded by Gary's thoughtful (but lengthy) business review of the year. All of this good stuff, coupled with an MM Board summary, service awards, new people introductions, etc., consumed at least forty minutes, during which time Santa sat steaming in his elegant red velvet costume. Finally, Santa couldn't take it any longer. Seated in the front row by the podium and having lost a few pounds of sweat, he said to the on-droning Randy, "Knock it off, Jensen. Santa's dying in here . . . and besides, he's got to pee!" The General Meeting went bananas.

There was only one time that I wanted to join Bailey in costume. I saved this appearance for the evening before the 1992 shareholders' meeting, when the Chief Executive Officer title was passed on to Bailey. It was too good to miss. We had been called the "Buzz & Bailey Show," so we appeared dressed as Laurel and Hardy! Bailey, the shorter of the two of us, asked me, "I guess there's no chance that I'll be Laurel, is there?"

Bailey and I had a lot of fun during the almost six years we were a team. And a team it was. It felt somewhat like what in basketball is called a "full-court press." This is performed when you don't have much time, and you want to put full pressure on your competition.

The key to the Company success in the late 1980s and early 1990s has been the focus that each of our managers has put upon improving operations. My own simple business philosophy is, "You must be successful, and you should have fun doing it." One without the other is no good, and there simply is no reasonable alternative.

Bailey and I agreed that our business was trying to do too many things at once. We needed to drive the winners and fix or divest the losers. Our Executive Committee agreed on a one-page mission statement, which helped keep us on focus. Of vital importance to our Company's success and the future of our people is our independence. For that reason it has always been important for our employees to own stock – stock in their own company, stock in their own future. This in turn helps them focus.

Divestitures have been made to strengthen our Company. The biggest one was McCormick Properties. This subsidiary was not sold because it wasn't doing well, but because it represented potential high risk to our continuing independence. There is no great secret responsible for the success of McCormick during the period of 1988 through 1992. It involved having the right person in the right job, focusing on what was important, and making a total commitment to being the best. Total quality management and global sourcing have been consistently improved under Bailey's leadership and dedication.

I was rather amazed when I was called on to address our McCormick/Schilling national sales force shortly after being elected President. When I stated that I simply wanted us to be the best, I received a loud, standing ovation. This was a surprise, and it taught me once again that the ultimate value of our Company is its people. Because we want to be the best and are willing to work at it, we are the best.

We have been rewarded in many ways, but to have the best performance in the stock market of any food company over a five-year period is something all our employees can be justly proud of. They did it.

Recently, one of the areas receiving top management's intensive care has been the globalization of McCormick. The bridge from being a company with an International Division to one that thinks globally is an important one today and will play a large part in the Company's future. Many people think that international travel is exotic and interesting, but it is also tiring and difficult; and it's important to understand local customs and cultures.

Ted McLendon built our Australian business from its beginnings. On his first trip to Seoul, he was treated to an evening at a traditional Korean geisha house. Following an hour of folksongs and dances, accompanied by an incredible mixture of Oriental and Western musical instruments, "dinner" was served. It consisted of a large variety of assorted hors d'oeuvres spread out on a large knee-high table, around which the group was seated, on the floor of course. A geisha girl was assigned to each guest with the principal duty of force-feeding her assigned charge, using the ubiquitous chopsticks. Conversation was thus frequently interrupted in mid-sentence when one's geisha might decide the time had come to inject another offering into the guest's often unprepared mouth.

Midway through the feast, Ted suddenly encountered great difficulty in swallowing a particular morsel that his geisha had shoved into his mouth. The more he chewed the bigger it got. He finally decided to pray and swallow before it was too late. Ted also made a mental note to avoid any future offering of that particular "delicacy." However, being curious as to its identity, Ted asked his hostess. Many explanations and giggles later, Ted realized that he had just eaten his first – and last – piece of a reproductive part of a water buffalo!

Ted flew into Tokyo a few years later to join Jack Caffey, then McCormick's International Vice President, in anticipation of the annual meeting with our Japanese joint venture. Checking into his hotel late Sunday afternoon, he found two messages waiting. One was from Caffey, inviting Ted to one "last" Western-style dinner before being thrown into the cycle of Japanese cuisine. The other message was from a long-time Japanese friend and associate. This was also a dinner invitation, which expressed the hope that Caffey could join them. Caffey declined because he knew from experience that this would involve an introduction to new, exotic Oriental "delicacies." Ted accepted the Japanese friend's invitation rather than Caffey's. Midway through the meal, Ted again dared to ask what they were eating. His friend smiled and informed him that he was again eating reproductive parts, this time from a female pig. He added gratuitously that "Jack didn't enjoy 'fun food' like the two of them did!"

Ted McLendon also had dining experiences with Jack Caffey's predecessor, Don Hallam. Back in 1966 they visited Manila together for a conference with Ruben Sy, our Philippine distributor. After preliminary discussions, Ruben suggested a break for lunch. Being Chinese, Ruben was anxious to show off the best that Manila had to offer in the way of Chinese cuisine. Being also most courteous, he insisted that Don select the dishes. When Don suggested chow mein, Ruben explained with some reluctance that chow mein was an American dish. Don thereupon selected chop suey, which, of course, is also American and was unavailable.

The next year Hallam visited again, this time in Tokyo to participate in ceremonies commemorating the signing of a license agreement with the Lion Corporation, which was later to become our Japanese joint venture partner. On the Friday night following the official ceremonies, Ted McLendon, Don Hallam, and Don's wife, Jerry, were taken out by our Japanese associates to celebrate less formally. Having been through the routine several times previously, Ted assured Hallam that come midnight, the clubs would close and the threesome would be deposited back at their hotel in time to recuperate for the next day's programmed tour of the countryside. Accordingly, they paced their liquid intake on the assumption that the last toast would be at midnight. To their chagrin, they learned that the midnight closing rule could be quite flexible for special occasions. Don Hallam was never famous for being able to hold a lot of alcohol. He had extremely long legs, which on occasion became quite rubbery.

The group returned to the hotel well after 3:00 A.M. The hosts' schedule for Saturday's countryside tour dictated an 8:00 A.M. departure, so Ted resurrected himself at 7:00 A.M. and struggled down the hall to Hallam's room to join Don and Jerry for breakfast. Ted felt that it was rather miraculous that he had negotiated this far. On reaching Hallam's door he was suddenly "inspired" to fall to his knees and scratch on the door, instead of employing the conventional knock. The door slowly opened, exposing a weary Don, also on his knees! Stalemate.

Here's a letter I received from Jack Caffey, now happily in retirement down in North Carolina:

> **One night stands out most vividly. It features Alex Orr, who was our U.K. Sales Manager. As the saying goes, "It was a dark and stormy night, etc." That afternoon Alex and I had successfully pitched our program for the big "McC"**

to the Managing Director of Fine Fair Markets in England and got the order to go into 172 stores. Upon returning to the office, where by my edict there was no booze permitted (there being no "Fifth Wheel Club"), I broke out a small bottle of wine of the country (scotch) to toast our "jolly good fortune." Not to be outdone, Alex produced a jug when a good friend of McCormick's showed up, Horace (Horie) Crouch of United Glass. Horie had helped us from early days in setting up our U.K. packaging. I must mention that it was not a surprise that Horie rapped on our door at the very instant that Alex cracked his wee jug. Horie had the well-earned reputation of a foxhound on the first instant the familiar scents of old malt whiskey found his sensor.

After an appropriate interlude toasting our astonishing good fortune, we set off for dinner. We chose the White Elephant on Curzon Street, Mayfair, which the other Barons of marketing and commerce frequented. I recall that it was raining, and West End traffic at any time was something right out of Dickens, except with motorized hacks.

We were in convoy, Alex, Horie, and I, when Alex hit the rear of the cab just in front of him. London cabbies rate their cabs right up there with their "fish and chips" or their "bangers and mash" as fond objects of their affection. As the cabbie was about to alight from his rig, Alex, with "hair-trigger reaction" at the prospect of battle that must have come directly from the genes of Robert the Bruce, beat the cabbie to the first exchange and roared, "What the bloody hell's the idea of backing into me in this traffic?" Before the surprised driver of the cab could reply appropriately, a bobby came over, his shoes pointing to "ten past ten." Realizing he was outnumbered by Alex, he told the hack to get along then and apologized to Alex.

A rather boozy dinner followed, at or near the conclusion of which Alex just missed the blancmange as his head hit the table. With our high spirits of success earlier that afternoon, it capped the day.

There are many other events of course over a 37-year career and many people with whom one has shared funny, often hilarious events: C. E. Miller getting caught in the oversized seat in his new toilet; R. C. Crampton the night the drive shaft fell out while he was driving his first Cadillac up Market Street, a Cadillac Bob had bought just that day from C. E.; Joe Braun after a couple of shooters looking like the Cape Hatteras lighthouse; Buzz holding up the plane for Baltimore at the San Francisco Airport while he changed his socks from summer weight to winter weight, etc. All I hope may add to your memories of life in the "spice factory."

I accompanied the Vice President - International, Jim Albrecht, on a trip from Scotland to Dissen, Germany. We were visiting our friend Dieter Fuchs, an associate with a spice business in Germany. Dieter later bought the Baltimore Spice Company, a competitor of ours in the industrial spice business.

Dieter had made his Lear jet available to us for the trip. My wife, Jimi, was with us also. As we were winging our way toward Germany, Dr. Albrecht stared out the window and exclaimed, "Did you see that jet just go by us? That's got to be the fastest plane in the world! It went by like we were standing still." I said, "Doctor, you idiot, that plane was going in the opposite direction. You're riding backwards!" Jim was mortified. When we landed, I wanted to talk to the German pilots. To make casual conversation, I asked them what the drinking rules were for German pilots. "Ah! Drinking rules. Haf you not heard what the Lufthansa captain said to his co-pilot as they neared New York on a transatlantic flight? 'You must stop drinking the wine now because in one-half hour we will be renting an Avis car.'"

That night we went to Dieter's home for a wonderful dinner, but Jimi was shocked when we left her alone with Dieter's wife, Ushi. Jimi politely apologized for not being able to speak to Ushi in her native language. Ushi responded quickly, "Oh, Jimi, it is no problem. You won the war. If we had won, you would be speaking German all the time!"

Hank Kaestner, who has flown all over the world in the pursuit of spices and vanilla, one-ups the Lufthansa story.

Hank and vanilla-bean supplier Nick Gaffney were flying an

Air France 707 from Paris to Kenya. At 35,000 feet over Egypt at 2:00 A.M., Hank went to the head. He looked out on the flight deck to see no pilot, no crew, and women's undergarments draped all over the instruments in the cockpit.

Hank went back to his seat to tell Nick that no one was flying the plane. Nick, thinking Hank was kidding, went forward himself. One of the male crew, naked and covered with foam, jumped in front of him and pulled the curtains closed as a girl screamed. Nick returned to his seat white as a sheet. Later the pilot explained, "Just flight initiations for a crew member."

Pilots aren't the only ones who clown around. How about the following story about Ted Foti and Randy Jensen:

> In the course of one of several trips to the West Coast during the period of integrating the Stange Company acquisition into McCormick, Ted Foti "acquired" and kept in his briefcase a set of earphones for a United Airlines DC10.
>
> His feeling at the time was that having paid full fare for the flight, it was unfair to have to pay $4.00 more to rent a headset. Later, he mentioned it to Randy Jensen, who was appalled at the idea of stealing headphones. Ted explained that he would, of course, return the headphones when he finished traveling at the end of his career. Subsequently, Randy Jensen reviewed the idea, and deciding that it made sense, acquired a similar set of headphones to keep in his briefcase.
>
> Later, on another cross-country flight to California, Randy and Ted were sitting on opposite sides of the aisle from one another. The lady next to Randy rented headphones. The breakfast was served and cleaned up as the attendants prepared for the movie. At that point the lady was unable to find her headphones. She signaled the flight attendant and told her the problem. Spontaneously, Ted said to the flight attendant, "Miss, you should check in that man's briefcase," pointing to Randy. "I believe that he took the woman's headphones and put them in his briefcase."
>
> Randy was extremely uncomfortable because in his briefcase was a set of headphones for which he had no rental receipt. The flight attendant issued another set of

headphones to the lady and went on about her business.

Meanwhile, Randy kept looking across the aisle and giving Ted Foti the evil eye. Ted responded by opening up his briefcase and surreptitiously removing his headphones along with some paperwork, which he dutifully performed during the course of the trip, watching the movie only intermittently. Randy had to sit through the whole trip unable to open his briefcase, unable to take out his headset, and, of course, unwilling to spend $4.00 to rent another headset. You never know when the evil hand of a practical joke is going to reach you.

And then there's the Company plane incident as related by George Clausen, our "Mr. Garlic":

In the early 1960s, Bob Crampton, Harry Wells, Doug Reed, and I were flying to El Centro, California to inspect the onion fields. After an early flight and a long hot day, we took off for the San Francisco Bay area. The plane would only hold the four of us plus the pilot, so I sat in the co-pilot seat as a passenger.

The flight was smooth and everyone had nodded off when I reached down to move my seat backward a bit. Or so I thought. What I had really done was pull a knob which shut off the fuel to the right engine. As the engine began to sputter and lose power, we fell off slightly to the right, and at once the rest of the passengers came awake!

Our pilot, Bud Davis, knew exactly what happened. Power was restored in just a few seconds, and the plane continued to fly smoothly on "straight and level." As you can imagine, I was very emphatically instructed to fold my hands, keep them in my lap, and not touch *anything* for the rest of the flight.

Bob Crampton went to Baltimore a few days later and was laughing about the experience in the Tea House at Light Street. John Curlett happened to be in the group and apparently got pretty uptight over the incident, particularly with top executives Bob Crampton, Harry Wells, and Doug Reed all in the same plane. Shortly thereafter, a Corporate edict spelled out who could and could not travel together in a small plane, particularly when George Clausen was present!

Obviously, many of the great memories come from traveling times. The stress of travel and the boredom of waiting must bring out the best (or worst) in us.

Chuck Mattern, Advertising Manager, had a tough trip the year that we presented new graphics for our packaging and a face-lifting for our "Mc" logo. The McCormick Division marketing crew attended six regional sales meetings and each time put on a pretty exciting program for the salesmen. When in Dallas, planning for the transportation to Atlanta, the group was asked if anyone would like to take advantage of one available ticket on an earlier flight.

Mattern jumped at the thought of getting away from the intensity of the group for a night and volunteered for the ticket. Carter Parkinson, then Vice President of Sales and Marketing, said, "Fine, and incidentally, since you are going early, you can take all the equipment with you so it will be there and set up when the rest of us arrive." The "equipment" was packed in sixteen boxes!

Chuck had been the butt of group devilment on the trip anyway, and this only proved again that when you are on a bad roll of luck, you sometimes can't do anything right.

These meetings included a question-and-answer panel at the conclusion of the presentations. The first meeting had been in Chicago. In his advertising presentation, Chuck had made the statement, "This is not the Pandora's box," following his ad agency-provided script. The statement didn't seem to fit or really make sense, and several of Chuck's associates pondered the question of whether Chuck really knew the meaning of what he had said.

So . . . in the written questions from the floor, out came a question addressed to Chuck: "What is a Pandora's box?" Chuck obviously didn't know the answer and did a fairly masterful job of deflecting the question and changing the subject. We couldn't believe it when Chuck's script at the next meeting in Dallas included the same reference to "Pandora's box." So . . . the question was sneaked into the salesman's question box again.

The same result ensued as Chuck parried the question. Again

and again at each meeting, the statement, the giggles, the question, and the non-answer repeated itself.

After the Baltimore meeting, there was one meeting left – New York – and I was going to miss it. Chuck took me aside and said very confidentially that he had figured out that one of the rascals from the home office had been planting that question on Pandora's box and that he was sorry I was missing the New York meeting because he was ready for the S.O.B.'s.

He had asked the ad agency to prepare a lengthy, professional and very humorous answer to the question. Chuck couldn't wait to finally get his revenge. But a strange thing happened at the New York meeting. Would you believe, the question never came up?!

Some years back, we desired an improvement in our vanilla package graphics. Our other extracts sported beautiful vignettes of lemons, oranges, strawberries, etc., but we had been unable to properly depict vanilla graphically. The vanilla orchid didn't seem to work, so our package had remained without vignette.

One day, an artist from Princeton, New Jersey visited, looking for a project. Now this guy was a little strange and definitely "light in the loafers." We gave him $750 and an impossible assignment: to create a vanilla design.

Incredibly, this fellow came up with the beautiful vanilla drop that is still used on our package today. He employed a Chinese artist who was particularly good at drawing water droplets on leaves and flowers.

We all thought that this simple and direct approach was great and wanted to go forward with it. However, Marketing Vice President Bud Weiser was out of town on an extended trip. When he returned, we presented this breakthrough to him, only to find that he had great reservations about using it. He said, "We have been promoting the *magic spoonful* of McCormick vanilla' for years, even on national television, and using a drop rather than a spoonful on the packages denotes that one should only use a *drop* of vanilla." I was quite disappointed and wrote to our artist friend for help, telling him of Bud's concern.

Two days later, I received the greatest telegram I've ever set my eyes upon. It went like this:

> **Even the village idiot would not think that a drop of vanilla denotes that that is all that one should use. If you do not allow me to breathe creatively in your behalf, our project cannot be successful.**

We allowed him to "breathe creatively!"

The value of a good telegram had its effect on me personally. I had purchased a sailboat that was complete, less a missing "dog" (fastening latch) for the forward hatch. A very minor fitting, but important in case of heavy weather when the hatch might come open, exposing the boat to much seawater.

I had tried for three months by phone, by letter, and face to face with the Grumman Company's Regional Sales Manager and his traveling companion, a company lawyer, to obtain this little fitting. A telegram finally got action. It read:

> **If not for my sake, if not for your sake, for Christ's sake, send the dog.**

The dog arrived two days later.

Meeting all the Grumman, Pearson division executives the next year at the New York boat show, I found that I was a celebrity there!

We've mentioned a number of times the involvement of industrial psychologists in our history.

Down under in Australia, our department heads have historically held periodic meetings, which were informal and open enough for any manager to bring up any subject of interest. At one of these meetings, one manager asked the others for their frank opinions on the value of psychological profile testing. The marketing manager proceeded to relate how he, desirous of discovering his true "inner self," had paid for an in-depth analysis at an East London clinic. When asked to reveal the findings, he "sheepishly" admitted that the clinic's bottom-line conclusion was that he was best suited to be a *shepherd!*

So much for the evaluation of marketing talent.

An important ingredient in any company's life is a financial plan. Even more important, in my opinion, is a clear vision of what your company should be; a tight mission statement; objectives that you intend to exceed; and, most important, the right person for each job. If you are in a good industry, create the right motivational atmosphere, and continually stretch your desire for success, then you are in all probability going to be a winner.

Tom McCord was Vice President and Treasurer of McCormick. He later took an assignment as Chief Financial Officer of our complex International Division.

While the Company was entering its fourth consecutive year of truly outstanding results in 1991, and while our stock performance was the best in the entire food industry, we wrestled with budgets and financial plans. During one of these sessions, Tom suddenly exclaimed, "Our financial plan is bullshit!"

This broke me up, and the meeting adjourned. Not wanting to tinker with our luck of exceeding our aggressive financial plan for successive years, I never asked Tom to substantiate his proclamation. In my mind, his remains one of the great quotes in our history.

One of the wonderful "outside" characters of our Company has been Dr. Ted Woodward, who has been in charge of our medical program for many years. We look to him for guidance concerning the health of our people, and Ted has always displayed a high interest in our Company. He is a special guest at our Christmas Multiple Management Board party in Hunt Valley. He's a very empathetic man and an excellent doctor. He also has a great sense of humor.

Just as Ted was about to sit down for dinner while attending the Christmas party, he was approached by an employee, who was very excited and demanded that Ted look at his infected leg, which had him very concerned. Ted, annoyed by the intrusion into his evening of relaxation, brushed off the frightened employee and asked him to "call on Monday." This answer didn't suffice, and the employee said, "Well, what will you do?" As Ted turned his back and sat down at the dinner table, he said, "We'll have to amputate!"

Many years ago, C.P. was guest of honor at a Schilling and

PEPPER PEOPLE

Gilroy party at the Fairmont Hotel in San Francisco. Gilroy President George Clausen, as a token of esteem, made a presentation to C.P. and hung a wreath of garlic around his neck. George had forgotten that C.P. was terribly allergic to garlic and despised it. C.P. was gracious about the event, but with all the needling from his associates, George worried for several weeks about his future.

C.P. would be proud to know, however, that I inadvertently got back at George many years later – in fact, in the spring of 1992.

Jimi and I built a retirement house in Florida, as did George and Sharon. As our house was nearing completion, we invited George and Sharon for the night as our first guests. Now I inherited my father's distaste for garlic but know how much George and Sharon thrive on it.

So when they arrived and it came time for dinner, I told George that we would cook steaks on the outdoor grill. I'd cook ours and he could cook his and Sharon's just the way they like them – seasoned by George just the way they liked them.

We got out the steaks, started the grill, and marched to the newest and biggest custom-built spice rack in the United States . . . probably the world. Ninety-eight brand-new McCormick gourmet spices had just arrived from the spice capital of the world, Hunt Valley.

I got off to a fast start, grabbing the pepper, the Season All®, some mild curry powder, and a few other bottles. As I peppered my steak, I noticed that George hadn't gotten off the mark. He was still staring at the alphabetically arranged wall of spices, with a quizzical look on his face.

Suddenly, I was concerned. Could it possibly be that I ordered *no* garlic products for the set-up? No way! But George looked and looked and finally in a faint voice said, "Buzz, I don't think there's any garlic here." He was right. Search as we would, there was no garlic.

I apologized profusely, being very embarrassed. Here I am serving the garlic king of the world ninety-eight spices and no garlic. Of course, George is the complete gentleman, and Sharon

The Executive Committee reflects on McCormick's five-year record, best in the industry. The stock shot up five-fold.

(Seated l-r): Hal Handley, Vice President and General Manager of McCormick/Schilling Division; Carroll Nordhoff, Executive Vice President - Corporate Operations Staff. (Standing l-r): Jim Hooker, Vice President and Chief Financial Officer; Buzz McCormick, Chairman; Bailey Thomas, President and Chief Executive Officer; Gene Blattman, Executive Vice President and Chief Operating Officer.

the complete lady. George sprinkled some alternate seasoning on their steaks, and they politely declared that the dinner was "great," but *I know better!* C.P. would be smiling.

Most of the Company "characters" were long-term employees. But not all. Who will ever forget Ted Miles? He was CEO of the Stange Company when we acquired that maker of the famous Kentucky Fried Chicken "magic blend of herbs and spices."

Ted became a member of the Corporate Board of Directors for several years. Along with the sale of Stange, which he had been head of, Ted provided substantial humor to our top ranks.

He hated long meetings and loved liquid refreshments. His constant pleading of "This is very dry work" served to shorten many business sessions — mornings or afternoons.

While dozing off quite "soundly" during a Corporate Board Meeting, he was elbowed by an associate. Ted opened his eyes and stated that he was okay, just resting his eyes. "Yes," came the reply, "But your snoring is keeping the rest of us awake!"

Then there was Corporate Board Christmas dinner during the early 1980s. We were still sensitive to the Sandoz raid, which we had successfully fended, and cognizant of the rich assets which we had on our books in the form of our McCormick Properties' real estate.

Ted, sitting at Chairman Harry Wells's table, was overheard to ask Harry in a loud voice, "Are you worried about another raid on the Company?" "Naw," said Harry, not really wanting to discuss this heavy subject at the Christmastime rejoicing. Ted's booming voice then uttered, "Better keep your knees together, Old Boy!" The Chairman's silence and look of displeasure created giggles and several chokings at the adjacent table.

But possibly my most favorite story involves not an employee, but the former owner of T.V. Time Popcorn. Little Ben Banowitz, about 5 foot 6 and 72 years old, received a cold call from us asking if he would consider selling his company. We had identified popcorn as a compatible product for our business. Ben reacted to the question, "Why yes, why don't you come out to Chicago and visit?" Next morning I hopped TWA and after meeting with Ben, drove down to his Bremen, Indiana plant along with Ben's vice president.

Ben had owned a number of movie theaters in Chicago at the time television was clobbering Hollywood. With the knowledge that most theaters were only existing because of profitable popcorn sales, Ben put two and two together, sold his theaters and created T.V. Time Popcorn.

After the Bremen plant tour, the plant manager was overheard reviewing an employee survey with the Vice President. "If there was one thing that our employees could have, they would choose to extend the half-day Christmas Eve holiday to a full day," the plant manager explained. "Do you think that we could do that?" "&#@ No!" the Vice President explained. "Ben doesn't even know that they're taking off half the day!"

Ben Banowitz was a wiry little guy and on the trip back to Chicago, the Vice President told me that Ben had been a bantamweight boxer in college. He told me this rather incredible story: Several months ago, Ben was driving home from work when he noticed a car following him. Taking many short cuts, Ben found that his follower stayed right with him to his final destination. Ben turned into his apartment complex driveway and stopped. The pursuer pulled up right behind Ben and stopped. They both bounced out but Ben was quicker. He ran back to the other driver and delivered a perfect haymaker to the unsuspecting fellow's jaw. Down he went, out cold.

Somewhat proudly, the old man headed for the front door where the bellman came running out to greet him. "Mr. Banowitz, you just coldcocked the new tenant in 405!"

This book was written during the summer of 1992, the last year of the Buzz and Bailey team. Hopefully, it has provided some history and amusement, not only to those familiar with many of the characters mentioned, but especially to those who follow along and continue to build this great Company for the future.

Bailey and I have spent considerable time and effort in building a succession program to ensure that our company has the right mix of talent to lead McCormick into the twenty-first century. We have learned that finding talent is not difficult. Obtaining talent that is also unselfish and truly operates within the "2 for 1" spirit of team play is somewhat more difficult. It is mandatory that this spirit be preserved and cherished if McCormick is to remain a uniquely successful Company and long time winner!

May the fun times roll on!

Chapter Thirteen

Summary

"When all else fails . . . *laugh*. It won't solve the problem, but it will make you feel better."

Buzz McCormick, 1992